BLUE HOUSE

Ten Years on The Way Home

Veronica Braila

Published by KHARIS PUBLISHING, imprint of
KHARIS MEDIA LLC.

Copyright © 2022 Veronika Braila

ISBN-13: 978-1-63746-176-1

ISBN-10: 1-63746-176-3

Library of Congress Control Number: 2022946018

All KHARIS PUBLISHING products are available at
special quantity discounts for bulk purchases for sales
promotions, premiums, fund-raising, and educational needs.
For details, contact:
Kharis Media LLC
Tel: 1-479-599-8657
support@kharispublishing.com
www.kharispublishing.com

Table of Contents

INTRODUCTION

This is my family story, a story from 1927 in USSR. It was at the time when peasants who had a little more wealth than the middle class were called "Fists. Later, even those who had anything extra were called "Fists."

Here in my story you can find love, the fight for life, friendship, and endurance of the subconscious and destiny. You'll find a connection between truth in the sky and people's souls, and the most important thing, inner power. The power of humanity was hidden in all of us, without us knowing it. I couldn't feel this power in the beginning. Only later in life did I realize that I carried a power in me that could help me navigate through my journey, through tears and pain, and through patience and faith. Also, this book is not for everyone. Like some great paintings, many will not understand it, while others will see it and cry.

Veronica Braila

Piece by piece, I put myself together by finding myself between people and nature. I put together my mind, soul, and body. Just as I proved to my mind that the soul exists, I also proved to my soul that God exists, and God will give me life in a body. This is hard to understand when your mind is preoccupied with the fear that the next day you will just get crazy.

This story has been written over years; it has been written like a piece of beautiful music that stays inside the atmosphere, flies everywhere here on Earth with us, and comes back to our soul, maybe in different colors but the same composition. The timeframe does not matter; what really matters is that everybody feels the same about passion, parting, betrayal, love, hope, fears, or patience in any time of history.

Sometimes, you don't know that something is coming to you. It could be a time for a turnaround in your life, even when you are happy and peaceful. You just don't know what is going to happen to you and you are not prepared; you are alone facing all the things, or somebody can be with you, but you wouldn't even know it. Perhaps in the last moment you can see people who are open and ready to stand by you. Perhaps you can see people ready to push you over a big precipice while you hear others saying: "Everything bad happens for the better!"

But in my view, nothing bad happens for the better. Bad things just happen. They should be viewed as bad and not the other way round. In most situations, when bad things happen, you face yourself. And this is important because it is time for you to grow up from those moments you keep asking: "Who I am? Is God real? Why did I come to this Earth? Is there life after death? Or is nothingness forever?"

I started respecting and appreciating my sacred time on this beautiful Earth.

We were living in paradise, 'til one morning, I woke up and realized that my destiny had thrown me so far that I came to the moment when my arms were my pillows, and my consciousness was my best friend. I learned to win my mind, to ask all the gods on Earth to be on my side and do things that would help me fight for my family and for me. At some point, I was a witch who prayed to God.

When I met him, I didn't know how my life would be with him. Precop was always confident in his actions and his decisions; he was fair and tolerant and always believed in friendship, in people, and in his work. He was a real leader, not a follower. From the first day I saw him, I admired him and couldn't get enough of him. His temperament, his love for everything and everybody, his love for work, and his love for family members were incomparable.

I was always there for him and always obeyed him. He knew how to direct and listen to people; in fact, everybody was running to him for advice. He looked so good, his face so lovely and sweet, and sometimes so serious that you would be afraid to ask him something. And when he entered any room, he would fill the whole space with his energy, his charisma, his laughter, and he could make anybody laugh. He didn't have to try to please people, it was natural for him.

***

This story is about how we went through the tragedy of Soviet village collectivization and dispossession from 1927-1939. Those were hard and unfair times. The laws were against people; people's voices were not heard, and if you were gaining strength and tried to say anything in your own right, immediately you would be punished. You had to obey, no matter your social or physical challenges, even if you and your family died of starvation. This was the application of decisive measures against the "kulaks," up to execution. ("Kulaks," also "Fists", were clearly defined: a peasant using wage labor in the economy.) To finally untie their hands, the authorities coined the term "Under Kulaks" ("under Fists"). Any dissatisfied collectivization could be attributed to this category, regardless of property status. According to archival documents, families sometimes fell under dispossession because they had two kettles for tea, they went to church too often, or starting in 1929, they killed a pig or sheep they raised in order to eat, thus preventing the livestock from becoming socialist property.

The cries of women, the crying of children, squandering property, lack of accounting - all this created the picture of night robbery. At the beginning of all this chaos, people resisted, but after the killing of about one and a half thousand Soviet workers, there was no way to the light. Many participated in the massacre on the soldiers' side; those were mainly peasants who were made up of stupid, envious, drunk, or ambitious young people. The pressure of that time was unbearable. People fought and survived as best they could.

The betrayal was unbearable from neighbors, friends, and relatives, from all people who sided with the soldiers, people who had nothing, and lazy, dumb, alcoholics. They did not understand that they would get nothing back from it, and their little brains heard: "Justice," and that was how they started fighting. But they never questioned themselves: *Against whom am I fighting? Why? Is that fair to take from others what they have accumulated over the years and with their sweat?*

I remember how Precop tried his best to save our lives and take us out of all this mess. After all these calamitous years came hunger and hopelessness. What was there to expect if everything was in the hands of the drunk and lazy people? People did not have time to understand the new laws. Some people didn't even know they were guilty. Everything was declassified and there was only one direction from the government. But people's spirits in those days were like a black rose that was never grown in other lands, only in the land where they were born.

Every morning releases an animal ahead of you! An animal named Faith, to direct you, to give you power, and always with a cold-as-a-rock look ahead. There is love and there is death. Life is worth living and love is worth waiting for, even though both are like a burning fire. Death reminds us that we are human beings, before religion, before our intellect, before our capital, and before our past. We are all equal in front of death. Love, I mean true love, is only between a mother and her child. Others have to learn from that, take an example from that love; that's love without reason. Everything in your life must flow and glow through your veins in no other way.

People you love, or people who deeply love you, may be far away, or maybe you don't even know where they are now. Yet you always can touch them in your dreams and mind, hold them, and warm them. A moment without them will pass, and one day you will brighten their way to you by calling upon your God every day to help you and help them.

This sounds so cold and crazy, but sometimes there is no other exit. Imagine years in a row with no holy days. Imagine an empty year when everything is not going the way it's supposed to go; everything is a mess and you are lost in this mess. There is just one gate and your mind is traveling so perfectly that you can open this gate any time you visit everybody you know, or you miss.

Isn't that amazing?

Through understanding the surroundings and the universe, I learned a lot from Precop, my husband. Sometimes, smart men lock up their wisdom. Precop was everything, a smart, wise, real man, a real father, and a real friend. There was so much love between us, so much patience, understanding, trust, and feelings. He was the leader in everything.

Before I met him, I was thinking it was so bad to live this life on Earth being a male. I was also thinking that men can't feel the tiny world; they don't see these beautiful butterflies, flowers, and colors as even interesting. *I mean, do they close their eyes to feel the sun's touch? Do they even know that you can feel it on the skin?* But not him, he took my hand and showed me even deeper feelings toward nature and people.

He was everything to me, and also he taught me to be everything to him. I didn't know there was another person like me, so deep, so beautiful. He was like an endless source of beauty for me. In fact, meeting him was a miracle.

CHAPTER 1

My father was the Ambassador of Russia and his name, Georgii Foka, was known by a lot of people. He was tall, a little full bodied, which earned him everybody's respect. We loved him a lot, to say the least. I grew up with "waiting" feelings, always waiting for Dad to come home from his work because he was always busy traveling and attending meetings in different cities and villages. His adventurous lifestyle encouraged him to speaking five languages. His job was to transport expensive icons, documents, and antiques from church to church. Despite this, we lived very modestly. My mom and my sisters and me, three kids, always waiting for him to come home and bring us some sweets and stories about his traveling. I remember how happy we were, screaming and running outside whenever we heard the noise of horses and carriages.

We'd exclaim, "Father is coming, father is coming!" Afterward, everybody from the house would rush out and jump into his arms. Usually, he was accompanied by four or more people. In those days, my mother was always cooking a lot of food. Our house always smelled of freshly-cooked food and was full of loud voices and conversations on those few days when Dad and the others were there.

One day, one of his friends gave him an icon. It was very beautiful and big, all made from platinum, maybe one meter big, with Mary depicted on it. It had a beautiful frame and corners and it hung on a wall in our living room. "In no case should you sell this icon!" said my father to all of us. "This icon is an inheritance," he added.

After three years, my father came home one day in his usual way, and we all were happy to stay on his lap listening to his story. He wasn't feeling good; he was sad, without the power and energy he'd had before. The next day, he woke up and told my mom, Maria, about his dream. She and I, who was also called Maria, had bad dreams too, so something quite bad was going to happen very soon. Dad had dreamt, too.

He hugged my mom and said, "I saw in my dream a lot of black dogs, and they tore me to pieces; I practically couldn't run away from them."

My mom's eyes filled with fear and tears and she looked at him and said, "You're not going anywhere. Please, I am begging you, please!"

She fell to her knees, screaming and crying, and hugged his legs, but she knew he would definitely go. His work was everything to him, although we all knew it was dangerous traveling at that point. Thieves always tried to rob his carriage, so his trips were usually made in secret.

I couldn't understand why my mother was acting like this. Nothing happened. Because of a dream, why? I didn't know that she had feelings in addition to Dad's dream.

Dad said, "I have to go; people are waiting. They know I am coming and I have to deliver my documents and the antiques I have with me." He added, "Get up Maria and be stronger. It is just dreams and nothing more." In his usual loving manner, Dad hugged her, kissed all of us, then he dressed and left.

In the past, people paid close attention to dreams and their interpretations. People were guided by dreams and signs.

In a few weeks, we got a letter stating that thieves robbed his carriage and killed all of his team. I was eight years old, and this was the first time I felt pain in my soul. It was a breaking, critical moment in my life.

I didn't know how to read it, but I took the letter from my mom and looked for a few seconds; I felt like I could burn it with my eyes. I couldn't understand how this piece of paper could bring so much pain to me and my family. I grew up in one day. I couldn't talk to my mom, she was so devastated. I couldn't talk to my sisters; they were so little they didn't even understand that they no longer had a father to love them. I was taking care of them. I stopped talking too much, when before, nobody could stop me. I thought endlessly with my gentle and fragile brain.

My mother was so weak; she didn't know what to do and she was crying day and night. Left with no options, she started to sell things from around our home to make money. Looking at her, I understood one important thing: women without love are not shining like a burning star. I learned that some wounds don't end, but always take away your mind.

Time flew; life was very hard. No one spared us, and no one helped us.

I especially remember one day at the end of February. It was cold outside and the sun shone; snow was everywhere and the glare almost made me feel blind. In the evening, we all came home, the kids from playing outside and my mother returning after a hard-working day. Tiredness was boldly written on her eyes. I was helping my mom around the house and also cooking for my sisters. I was the oldest one, and this was why they named me Maria, like my mother. We felt it was such a terrible hard time due to my father's death and my mom finding it extremely difficult to feed us. Worse still, we were wearing hand-me-down clothes and our mom worked from sunrise till sunset.

January 14 was my birthday and I turned sixteen years old. Like a gift from early in the morning, my mom gave me a few minutes of attention. She hugged me and planted a beautiful kiss on my forehead, then she stroked my hair and said, "Thank you, Maria, my oldest daughter, you have my name, but your temper is from your father. I love you so much!"

She had no time for us; in the evenings her hands were busy with my siblings, and I was very important to her, for her attention, her words, and her smile. I always tried my best to help her feel happy.

We lighted candles and positioned them everywhere in our home; we had no power at that time. The outside was already dark; everything seemed so calm and so usual.

Suddenly, a strong knock on our door interrupted the silence, and our door was small. This was after my father's death, and we had moved to this small house. To me, it seemed that whoever was knocking so hard and loud was trying to break the door. My two little sisters ran and hid under the table, and I did the same thing, even though I was already sixteen years old, my mother's strong girl with my father's temper. The table was facing our front door. My mom smiled at us; she didn't feel any danger. We were very poor. What could anyone want from us?

My mother opened the door. I remember how he came in; he stooped slightly because of our low door. He stepped in with his right foot and his boots were so shiny and new; nobody in our village had a pair of boots like that, at least I hadn't seen anybody. He was thin, tall, with a belt around his waist. He took off his hat as soon as he entered; behind him were two more men and his mother. Those men seemed like they were repeating all their moves after him, especially when he took his hat off. The lady was quiet and intelligent. Those men were his best friend and his cousin.

We were so surprised to see them in our house. We all knew them and they were from a wealthy family. His parents had farms, lands, gardens, horses, and a big mill, where everybody, even from other villages, came to make flour.

His face, his look, and his movements seemed so confident. Everybody was looking at him, even the men and the lady who had come with him, waiting for him to start a conversation. He looked around the room for a few seconds, bowed his head to my mother, and then he said with a calm and strong voice, "Good evening! My family and I arrived with good intentions to this house and this family…."

My mother was so confused, and at the same time, it seemed that she knew why they'd come. She got upset right after he said those words. She looked at all of them and they were looking at each other without any expressions on their faces. Usually, my mother was very friendly and happy with our guests, but that day she was looking different, confused, and lost. The man started the conversation very simply, stating, "I would like to marry your daughter Maria. I like her, I saw her several times, and every time I saw her, she was either laughing with her friends, or with her sisters; her laugh is so lovely. Her care for everything is so special, her green eyes are always sparkling with happiness. Even I know how much you struggle for survival. I am sorry, but she is different than everybody I know. She is special, and I promise I will love her and protect her for the whole of my life."

There was a deafening silence in the room; I could even hear the crackling of candles and my heartbeat. In fact, I stopped hearing anything for a moment. I could think about nothing. All of that Nirvana was interrupted by my mother, "Oh, kids, please come out from under the table!"

I came to and started gently pushing my sisters out. I followed, with my empty head down, and I was looking just at the floor. I rose and stood like a statue beside the table. My hair was braided in one long braid.

"Maria, go and bring some water and cut some bread on the table," continued my mother. We didn't even have anything to offer but I immediately went to the kitchen.

I was thinking that they had the wrong house address, because I was barely old enough to get married; I was still young. Besides, who would help my mother take care of my sisters? Inside, I had an odd feeling about the visitors and this situation.

Veronica Braila

"Please, sit down," said my mother, giving everybody chairs. As I strained my ears, I could not hear what they were talking about from the kitchen. Through the slightly open door, I could look at their faces. My mother was sad; she tried to smile a few times through all her sadness. She was looking at me through the same slightly open door. My little sister came to my mother, who hugged her and continued talking and playing with her curly short hair, and her eyes were full of tears. Strangely, Mom agreed on my behalf, without asking me further questions or talking to me. She agreed for me to marry him. I had such deep, empty feelings. I was so confused, so lost, and not ready at all for having a family. I wondered, *How come? I didn't even know him. My mother didn't even explain to me what marriage meant, or how kids were made.* I felt like I jumped into cold water and couldn't swim. I didn't even understand if I was breathing or not.

"Thank you for letting us into your house and listening to us," he said, and got up from the chair. He caught my eye. I was shaking, my face was pale, in one hand I had the plate with cut bread, and in the other hand I was holding the jug of water. I stopped as soon as I left the kitchen. His cousin and his friend got up right after him, his mother too; everybody was looking at me. I raised my chin a little. He was in his early twenties, twenty-four years old to be exact. His eyes looked like those of a grown man, very serious. There was an eight-year difference between us. I couldn't stop looking into his eyes; I had no control of my body at all.

"Good night to everyone," he said, shifting his eyes to my mother. "And again, thank you for everything." He was so polite and he left without looking at me one more time. My eyes followed him till my mother closed the door. Afterward, I felt like he was my power and my power had left me at that moment.

"You will get married soon, in a few months," my mother said. "Everything is going to be okay," she continued, without looking at me.

I went back to the kitchen, washed my hands, and went back to the living room. My mother held out her hands and started crying. At once, I quickly ran to her and hugged her. I was feeling better, and finally my breath started to be normal. I understood why she made this decision for me; she knew with him I would have everything; I would be strong and smart. Sadly, I couldn't even write or read at that time because I wasn't going to school. I just couldn't, I had to help my mother to take care of my sisters.

Everybody went to bed or acted like they were feeling sleepy. I was lying in the same bed with my little curly-haired sister, and my mom was with another of my sisters. I was holding her so close that I could feel her warm breathing on my face. I wanted to hug everybody in my family. I couldn't sleep all night; my brain was working, questioning me, and I couldn't wait till the morning to tell my friends that I would be getting married soon. I couldn't believe all this was happening to me, I wanted to share it with somebody, but I couldn't explain, not even to myself, how I was feeling.

"Oh, God!" I prayed, thinking I would surely lay awake until the morning light. "Please, make me sleep at least a little bit, and take me away from all of these feelings and thoughts."

After all fears, lost feelings, and anger, something new was starting in my heart. I didn't understand it, but all I felt was happiness. I told myself, *For now, I feel good; I hope my feelings are not lying to me, and I will have all these feelings all my life with this handsome man.* And right away, I remembered his stern face and I felt a little fear again; he had been looking too serious for me. I was a very funny girl, but I told myself, *It's okay, even though I don't know him, I hope he will be the prince of my life's story.* "Anyway, I can run away from him should anything feel wrong," I whispered to my little sister, who had a long time left to sleep. I was looking out the window waiting for the sun to rise.

The next day was Saturday, before my mother went to work. Her friend who was working for Precop's mama was in the kitchen cooking for his family and workers. She knew everything about him; she had heard what happened last night and came to commiserate with my mother. Of course, I jumped like crazy to hear, so I would not miss even a word of their conversation.

I asked the woman, "Tell me everything. What he likes, what he eats, what he drinks, and what he doesn't like."

She started laughing with my mother, then told me, "He likes to wake up early in the morning, by 5 am every morning when he has to. If he doesn't have to, he will find something to do. He takes a cold shower and goes for a walk when everybody sleeps. I asked him why he wakes up so early. He said that he likes to think at that time when everybody sleeps; the atmosphere is so clean and quiet that he can hear his heartbeat, his soul. After a walk, he comes home and everybody will eat together. He asks absolutely everybody if they have any problems, so he can fix them, even workers, not just family.

"His father passed away when he was about thirteen years old; he doesn't have a brother or sisters, and he loves his mother and respects her. His hobbies include working, reading, and helping people."

She stopped for a moment and I asked, "Did he have women before?

She smiled and said, "I wouldn't know if he had, because he is a kind person who would not just offend someone or leave someone with failed promises; he always keeps his word and promises. You are so lucky that he picked you."

My mother smiled to me and said, "He is lucky with my daughter, too." Then the woman continued as she touched my hair, "He first saw you when he was going home. I heard how he described you to his mother: you were with your sister and mother and were holding hands, eating cookies. He told his mother that he has found a person who would fill his soul till the end."

All this day long he was in my mind; I couldn't stop thinking about him.

The next day was Sunday and usually on Sundays we have a big fair where all the villages around come to buy or sell their goods, and there we could buy something. Usually, I would go just to look around, just for fun, and sometimes, we would just go to buy sweets. This fair was the only entertainment for me. I loved to go there!

Early in the morning, I saw Precop through the window, alone, by my home. I didn't know what I should do. Should I open the door, or should I call my mother? I looked at the table in our living room where I had hid that day and I said to myself, *No, last time you were looking so stupid, Maria. You will get married soon.*

Next, my mother saw him through the window too, and shouted, "Oh, he is here, I cannot believe it. Did he even go home last time that he came this early this morning?"

She was joking with me so I could relax a little bit. She went outside to him and almost knocked him down at the door, but he wasn't sure what to do.

"Good morning!" My mother said and opened the door quickly so he would not wake up my sisters so early in the morning with his knocking.

"Good morning, Maria! Can I please take Maria with me to the fair? I will bring her safely back. I want to talk to her. I never did before, I never came close to her before, but with your permission, I would love to spend some time with her." He was so serious and shy.

Shy? I smiled. *I guess without your friend and cousin you will feel a little bit different, hmmm?* I said to myself and smiled again.

"Sure, it is a good beginning," my mother said, smiling and looked at him.

He relaxed and smiled back at her. My mother came inside and left him to wait outside. I jumped and went to look for my scarf, my coat, my boots, and my mom was watching me keenly, watching how I ran back and forth with my stuff in my hands. I couldn't find the brush for my hair and had to wash my face.

"Wait for a second," my mother said with her soft voice as she hugged me again, held me softly and gently with such a motherly tenderness. "We all know his family; they are very nice people, their workers are always so happy working for them and Precop is a very educated, smart guy," said my mom. She looked at me with sadness and guilt. She didn't know if her decision was right or wrong, and I was only sixteen.

"Thank you, Mom. Don't worry, I like him," I said and hugged her tight. She felt happy and relaxed after the hug.

"Oh my God," I said, "he is here, I have to open this door." For a couple of seconds, I did not even dare to open the door. Finally, I opened it and he was looking at the door then. He looked into my eyes. He smiled as he admired me walking down the stairs, my hair was loose, and I had my scarf in my hand.

"Good morning, please," he said and raised his hand, showing his carriage for two people, with one black horse up front. I walked in front of him, and on getting to the carriage he took my hand. This was the first time he touched me. He helped me to sit and let go of my hand right away; his touch felt very light and gentle. Then he entered and sat by me, and I couldn't say a word, when before, nobody could stop my loud talking and laughter. I wasn't sure if I was breathing at that moment.

"How do you feel?" he asked quietly.

"All is good," I said, as short as I could answer him. He was looking at me the whole time, but I didn't dare to look him in the eye; I was very shy.

"Before I met you, I used to see a dream, with a woman in it, and the woman in my dream was my woman," he said. "We had kids and were living very happily together. Every morning after, I would ask God to make my dream a reality and show me that woman. I am the only child in the family and I like kids. My father passed away when I was thirteen years old, and he left so much to my mother, like farms and a whole lot of acres of land. His friends helped my mother and me to deal with everything; they took nothing from us, and they could have, if they had wanted, because we knew nothing about the farmland. He never involved us in any work or problems, which I think was a huge mistake, as he was doing everything by himself. From then, I learned how to trust, and sincerely help others."

He paused and got back to his dream, saying, "I used to see this dream once a year, and one day I was going home after work and I saw you with your sisters and your mother, eating cookies, and laughing joyously. Something happened to me that day. I felt it, like a click in my heart. Your sisters were running around you and you were catching them. You were laughing and so happy, and after that day, I stopped seeing that dream and started thinking about you."

He told me that story about himself that seemed like a fairytale to me. I tried to look at him out of the corner of my eye, but he was staring at me. I couldn't say anything. I was ready just to listen.

"I think my dream stopped because I had met my dream woman in reality," he continued. I tried to look at him again and say something, but I still couldn't. I just didn't know what to say. My heart was like a stone and I couldn't even catch my breath. My face was red and then pale. We finally got to the fair.

"Can I stay here?" I asked him.

He was a little confused, but he said, "Yes, if you will feel more comfortable here." He smiled at me with such a sweet smile, then he said, "I will try to come back as soon as I can." I watched him enter through the crowd; how he walked between people, talking, smiling, and buying something amazed me. I said to myself, *Oh, where were my eyes till now? He was here among people, but I was so blind.*

My breath became normal again and I saw him looking at me from far away, through all of the people there. I had so many unusual feelings. After about one hour, he came back to me, his hands full of different vegetables and cookies that he'd bought. He put those things in a small basket in the back of the carriage and got inside; he had a white cloth napkin with sweets in it and handed it to me. I picked out one sweet with a "Thank you!" and I tried again to look into his eyes, but he was looking so deeply at me, like he was looking directly into my soul. These emotions took away my breath again and made me lose control. I couldn't even eat that cookie he bought for me; it was melting in my hand because I held it too tight. I tried to look at him again and I saw how he was looking at my hand with that cookie.

"Please, try to relax and don't be afraid of me," he said so gently to me. Then he asked, "Do you know how to read?"

"No, I don't," I answered him. He was waiting for more explanation, like why I couldn't read, and would I like to learn. But he didn't ask me anything more till we got home. He gave me that space of being quiet, and letting my feelings talk with myself inside of me.

We got home and all my family members were waiting for us; my sisters were awake and immediately jumped on me like they hadn't seen me for a decade. He came inside after me, bowing his head like always, because of our low doorway. He looked so lovingly at me and at my family. After looking at me and hugging my sisters, he took all the vegetables and sweets he'd bought, smiled, then he put everything on the table.

My mother said, "Oh, you shouldn't have, thank you."

My little curly-haired sister asked, "Can I see what you brought?"

"Yes, yes," Precop said, smiling, then he looked at me and said, "I have to leave; I will see you soon. I will not be here; I have to leave for a while because of my work."

He looked at me as I almost interrupted him and said, "Thank you.

He left and my mom entered the kitchen, telling us, "I will make some tea."

My sisters started eating the cookies. I was so happy my eyes were glowing. I was daydreaming and everybody was looking at me as they were eating the sweets. I looked at my little curly-haired sister, but nobody could say anything. I couldn't explain why I was feeling the way I did. In fact, I barely hid my smile that was already popping out from somewhere inside of me. Maybe they were waiting for me to tell them about my little trip to the fair but nobody asked. All my family were just looking at me and enjoying the moment of happiness that was coming from within me. But I told myself, *He just jumped into my life like this; I can't understand why I feel he is mine.*

The next day started like all the days before. My mother went to work and I was home with my sisters doing all the work around the house. Later, I went out for a walk with my friends, taking my sisters with me, of course. I told my friends everything about Precop, how he came to my home, how he asked my mom for my hand, and we laughed about how I hid under the table scared and wild.

"That's it, I am getting married, and I will be busy with my husband and my future kids," I said on a lighter note.

I imagined: *how will I look as a married woman?* After my friends left, I gradually started to understand that everything in my mind disappeared and dissolved as he occupied all my thoughts. I told myself, *He will become my best friend, my family, my husband, my everything, and I want this.*

I was waiting for him every day and I got to understand one thing for sure: I was nobody without his love, without his story about his dream. I liked him from the first day I met him.

After a week, he came back from his trip and came to our house with a lot of sweets and gifts. He also brought some smoked plums with nuts, my favorites, and these were their products. His family used to bake and dry plums, apples, and apricots in a large oven and sell them. Everything he brought to our home was delicious and accepted wholeheartedly.

"Maria, I bought your wedding dress," said Precop.

He went back to his carriage and brought in a beautiful white dress, which I had never seen before. Everybody was happy with him, not only me. He was giving attention to everyone in my family We all liked him. We started waiting for his visits, which were as often as he could make them. We couldn't get enough of him. I think this was an example of a real man, for real men are known for showing care, attention, energy, regard, and giving their time.

He started supporting my mother and my family, which made my mother's burden much easier for her.

Before the wedding, I tried on that dress a hundred times, cleaned the mirror, and danced happily. I couldn't wait for that day. I was acting like a little princess; I had not felt like this for a long time. After I lost my father, nobody had shown my soul this kind of love. I was overwhelmed with such joy in my spirit that my mouth couldn't even explain my innermost feelings.

CHAPTER 2

The time for our wedding came; his family had prepared everything. My mother gave me a dowry with the icon of platinum, the one my father had brought.

She said, "This is the only thing I can give you! You will give that to your daughter or your son. Never sell it. I love you so much, my precious daughter."

We had our wedding and everything was so beautiful and easy. His touch was gentle, the sunset was so beautiful, and I was happy. I moved my belongings to his house; I didn't have that much at that time.

The first morning I woke up, he made me coffee and told me, "This house is yours now. Never allow anybody to take this from you; it is special for you."

He handed me the documents for the house and there was only my name written on them. Wow, it was beautiful and the biggest gift I ever had.

"I would like to see you all the time, from sunrise to sunset, here till the end of my life," he said, and kissed my forehead.

This house was magic, with big windows that let so much brightness into the rooms, and high ceilings, which were rare at that time. From our bedroom, we could see beautiful sunrises and sunsets, plus the valley around the gardens with different kinds of fruits and flowers that Precop himself had planted. Very soon this house became my soul, my place where I felt like I was inside of a holy place. I think this is the way everybody has to feel in their homes.

His love for me was so beautiful, which kept me skeptical that something might go wrong. He activated all the lights inside of me. He taught me one beautiful thing, telling me, "It doesn't matter what happens to you on earth, just look in the sky, and look at the stars. Go deep into the galaxy, and dream." Whenever he observed that I was sad, he would kiss me till I started smiling. His love was so beautiful.

When you meet love, you have to be happy and sad at the same time; you'll be happy because that is happening to you, and sad because it will end one day. Even if love lasts till the end of your life, sadness will be inevitable.

In my opinion, Precop put this house in my name because he wanted me to feel special, feel powerful, feel that I was everything to him, and feel that he trusted me.

Precop had a special room just for himself, with a lot of books and papers inside. Usually, if I had to look for him, I would just go there.

He loved silence, so with time, I started to like silence too. Sometimes, I would catch him looking at me from the window; I always was outside in the garden, or by the animals playing with them or feeding them or riding the horse he gave me; he also taught me how to ride. I fell in love with him so very fast that wherever we went, wherever we were, his eyes were looking only for me and mine were looking only for him. He had made a one-time decision, and I was so grateful that he chose me.

He started to teach me how to read and write, saying, "Maria, you have to learn how to read and write; it is very important. Otherwise, our children will find it difficult to cope with schoolwork whenever I will be away from home." He laughed and said, "You will find some books very interesting," He kept saying this to me and he would read aloud some of his books with very interesting stories before we would go to bed.

Very soon I got pregnant, but unfortunately, I lost the pregnancy. As a young girl, I didn't know how to deal with it, so I was doing things ordinarily that I wasn't supposed to do, like jumping, running, and carrying things. Occasionally, he would catch me and try to stop me by saying, "Don't do that anymore please!" But I wasn't listening to him. Precop was very upset with me; he was dreaming of having kids, and waiting, but I disappointed him. I lost the baby in my seventh month of pregnancy. I was in our garden, as usual, I was screaming and crying, blood gushing out everywhere, and it was a scary sight to behold, so he vowed to stand by me in my next pregnancy.

How could I do that to him? I couldn't speak with him for a while after that. He was working outside with his workers till late and I was waiting for him to come and talk to me, but he was short on answers and quieter than usual.

"Sorry," I interrupted one of our quiet diners. "Henceforth, I promise you I will always hear you and listen to you," and I started crying. He got up from the table and hugged me gently, saying, "I am sorry, it was a good lesson for both of us."

After some time, I got pregnant again and I delivered a boy. Precop named him Georgii, a name he had always liked for a boy and I agreed. Our son Georgii was our first child and he was getting all the love from us. Every day he spent time with Precop.

After three more years, I delivered our second son, Jacob. Every day they were together, and Precop was teaching them everything, telling them stories, reading books, teaching them how to ride a horse, how to hunt, how to swim, how to make flour in our mill, and importantly, how to write.

Georgii was very courageous and of a strong temper. Jacob was different and softer; he couldn't even kill a bug. Georgii and Jacob fought all the time. One time, Jacob was playing with a ladybug and Georgii stepped on it. There was a big fight that day.

In five more years, Georgii was eight years old, Jacob turned five, and I delivered our daughter Pauline. She was so beautiful and she had big blue eyes and blond curly hair. Precop gave me a gift, a golden necklace; it was round like a coin, with an inscription: THERE IS NO LOVE, AFTER MY LOVE. The two meanings of this inscription are: He will never love anybody else, and secondly, I will never forget his love for me.

Precop was so affectionate, hugging and kissing everyone over and over with so much love. The children were asking him questions over and over and he was responding to them, to all their questions, laughing with them, joking with them, and dancing together almost every evening. I couldn't get enough of watching his love for our kids and me. I was so happy, more and more because of him. Precop planted pieces of himself in all of us.

It's so good a feeling for a woman to have a man who loves her and her kids, to feel his power and energy just for her, and when he sees you nothing else around matters than to have you and your kids and his family come first, then his hobby, his job, and friends.

At the end of the summer of 1930, I saw Precop with his childhood friend Anatolii and how they walked quickly into his office from outside. Precop had a newspaper; usually, he always had a fresh newspaper with him. And I came right after him because they looked very strange and very serious and they didn't even see me. When I went into the room, I saw he was writing a letter.

"Something happened?" I asked Precop quietly, and after a few seconds, he replied, "Not yet, but it very soon will. Look at this…!" He handed over to me the newspaper – I breathed deeply.

On February 15, 1928, the newspaper, *Pravda,* for the first-time published materials exposing the "Kulaks" (called "Fists" because of fighting back), reporting on the difficult situation in the countryside and the widespread dominance of the rich over the peasantry in the localities; they were found not only among the villagers exploiting the poor, but also inside the party, leading several communist cells. Messages were published about the destructive activities of the kulaks– revealing the kulak elements, as local secretaries did not let the poor and farm laborers into the local branches of the party.

On February 2, 1930, was issued the order of OGPU USSR NO 44/21{37}. It stated:

In order to organize the elimination of the Kulaks as a class and to decisively suppress all attempts by the Kulaks to counteract the Soviet government efforts to socialist reconstruction of agriculture, primarily in areas of continuous collectivization in the future, the

Kulak, especially its rich and active counter-revolutionary party, must receive a crushing blow.

The Order provided the "counter-revolutionary and rebel organizations and groups" and the "most malicious"– that's the first category to which we were assigned. The Kulaks (Fists) were the most active, opposing and frustrating measures of the party and the authorities in the socialist reconstruction of the economy. The Fists were fleeing from areas of permanent residence and going underground, especially those associated with active White Guards.

The Kulaks/Fists were the active White Guards, rebels; they were former white officers, repatriates, and showing counter-revolutionary activity, especially on organized order.

Active members of church councils and all kinds of religious communities and groups actively manifested themselves. Kulaks/Fists were the richest moneylenders, speculators, former landowners, and large landowners. Families of those arrested, imprisoned in a concentration camp, or sentenced to be shot, were to be expelled to the northern regions of the USSR, along with their Fists; they were to be evicted during the mass campaign, along with their families, taking into account the presence of the able-bodied.

On January 30, 1930, the Politburo of the Central Committee of ALL-Union Communist Party of Bolsheviks adopted the well-known resolution on measures to eliminate kulak farms in the area of continuous collectivization. According to this decree, the Fists were divided into three categories:

*First category: a counter-revolutionary asset, the organizer of terrorist acts and uprisings.

*Second category: the rest of the counter-revolutionary assets of the richest kulaks and semi-landowners.

*Third category: made up of the rest of the Kulaks/Fists.

Heads of Kulak families of the first category were arrested and cases of their actions were referred to special triunes consisting of representatives of the OGPU, or police, regional committees of the Central Party of the Soviet Union (CPSU), and the prosecutor's office. Families of the first and second categories were subject to eviction to remote areas of the USSR, or to remote areas of this region (territory, republic) for special settlement. Fists assigned to the third category settled within the district on lands specially designated for them outside the collective farm massifs.

The counter-revolutionary kulak asset was to be liquidated by imprisonment in concentration camps, including the organizers of terrorist acts, counter-revolutionary actions, and insurgent organizations, before applying the supreme sentences in relation to the first and second categories: Send sixty thousand to concentration camps and evict one hundred and fifty thousand Kulaks/Fists to uninhabited and sparsely populated areas with the calculation for the following regions: Northern Territory – seventy thousand families; Siberia – fifty thousand families; Ural twenty to twenty-five thousand families, and Turkestan –twenty to twenty-five thousand were expelled for agricultural work or industry.

According to the order of the OGPU NO 44.21 of February 6, 1930, the operation began to "seize" sixty thousand Kulaks/Fists of the "first category." Already from the first day of the operation, the OGPU arrested about sixteen thousand people, and on February 9, 1930, twenty-five thousand were arrested.

The government wanted everyone to be equal and work for a collective farm. No one knew what all this would lead to. People were fighting against this law with all the power they had. Churches were helping them accumulate money and information; everything was given to people to go against the government. After that, the government started to go against the churches and against religion.

Atheism, as a worldwide tenet denying religion, was not being formally proclaimed as an element of state ideology in the USSR, but it was actively supported by party and state bodies However, there came the complete elimination of organized religious life and the official prohibition of religion.

Precop was fighting with them from 1929 when we saw it for the first time published in the newspaper. He sent thousands of letters everywhere he deemed possible. There were different congregations in the church and people didn't want to agree with the government.

The leader of the USSR, Joseph Stalin, described 1929 as the year of the "Great Breakthrough." This year, the country had undergone significant changes in its domestic, political, and economic course, associated with the rejection of the New Economic Policy, forced collectivization, and industrialization.

Now, all this chaos was knocking on our doors; they were coming closer and closer to our territory at the end of the summer of 1930. All the people believed that they could do something and push this political misunderstanding and illogical dispossession back, but that was just impossible. Stalin was very hard on people; there was no explanation to even hear, no way to even come and read the report and start talking. These reports were ridiculous and about nothing, but who cared? The goal was to take everything, and if you tried to say something, they could even take your clothes, judging that you had too many of them.

Imagine you raise animals, get used to your animals for years, and somebody just forcefully took them from you; legally, the same thing was applicable with lands, harvests, everything you worked for for years belongs to everybody, not to you only, even though you were the only ones who worked hard for it. It was complete absurdity and chaos.

CHAPTER 3

Beginning of September 1930, I was bringing the food for my workers on the land when I saw an army passing by. I quickly ran home, calling out, "Precop! I saw a big army with black horses passing by." I explained to him how they looked, described what they were wearing, and which direction they were going, as he asked me all the details.

He told me, "Maria, put all the clothes for the kids and us in a bag, take winter clothes too, just make them ready, we have to be prepared!"

After he told me that, he went out to inform his friends and relatives about it, and what they had to do. He also went to check where the army stopped and he wanted to find out what information they had, from where they would start and when. Precop caught a soldier that was behind everybody and acted like he was one of the militants against the Kulaks/Fists and collected basic information from him. He learned that he had two to three days before they would settle down somewhere, get the lists of who had more and who was who in that region, and find someone who would point out those people. Many villains could do that, worthless people who craved power. This did not prove to be problem to find such villains.

I started packing everything as he told me. My hands were shaking and for a while I got so scared for my kids. Immediately, I went outside and started screaming their names, "Georgii come home right now, Jacob come home right now please, and play inside the house." I held little Pauline in my arms and all I could feel was fear inside of me, blocking my mind, and at the same time pushing me to do something, but I had no idea what to do.

Precop came home that night and I was waiting for him more than ever. As soon as he got inside, I started asking him, "What did you find out? What are we going to do now?"

He said, "Tonight, Maria, we will sleep at home; tomorrow, I don't know. They are bad! I'll have to take my mother to your mother's home; they will live together for a while."

I put everybody to sleep. I tried to fall asleep but it was impossible. Our boys were already asleep and I lay down by Pauline and started watching her sweet sleep; she was sleeping so calmly, her eyelashes, her hair, her lips were so sweet that night, and I couldn't get enough of her. Kids are a big, beautiful gift from angels, so clean, and so innocent. I was so scared for my kids, and for my husband. That night, Precop was back and forth, checking our windows. It was so light outside. The moonlight was shining in all the windows. I fell asleep for a few hours, after all this fear and stress and worries.

The next morning when I woke up, right away I started to look for Precop. He was in his room, sitting at his table, and writing something. I said, "Precop, I am scared. What's going to happen with us?" I hugged him from the back, my voice very soft.

He said, "Maria, we will have to move in with some of my relatives and live there for a while in another village. Although it will take a while for us to get there, the soldiers will need time to get there, too. I heard they are taking village by village, city by city, randomly, but they are more concentrated in villages. It is not going to be easy, however, we will change our names, and with money we can live in any city where nobody knows us. The most important thing is to get out of our village as soon as possible."

I gasped when I heard that. I didn't know it was already too late to run. Precop knew that it was already hard to get out of the village; soldiers were already everywhere. He told me, "Maria, the icon from your mother, it is better to hide it. They are against the religion, plus it is platinum. They're saying that there is no God and trying to change people's opinions about their religion and turn them into atheists so that there will be no churches and no place for people to communicate. In all this travail, just keep calm. Only take bread from my hand and I will decide how much I want to give you."

He took me in his arms and threw me playfully on the soft seat in his room and lay by me, saying, "You know I heard a story about Stalin that slipped out from his people. One time, Stalin gathered his people around him and also brought a chicken with him. The chicken was alive, and he began to pluck feathers from her and the poor chicken was covered in blood. Then he threw the chicken on the floor and threw grains near her and the chicken ran and started to eat. Stalin told the people, "Look at her, I hurt her, till she bled, but she's still coming to me because I am the one who is feeding her. There is something about people with gentlemen's hearts."

I stayed quietly by him, not knowing how to relate to this story, so I leaned against him and hugged him tightly. He said, "Maria my love, always have God inside of you and pray; whatever they do or say about politics doesn't matter concerning God's existence. He is a big power inside of us and He is working for us. Many books are about His power inside of us; we don't know any other way to use it. We just pray, we don't know how to name it, and we call upon God for help." He kissed my forehead then my lips.

Throughout the day, Precop was somewhere outside with the workers, Anatolii, and other of his friends. I was watching our kids and cooking. I couldn't let them play far from me and I had to see them every five minutes. When it was dark outside, I put the kids to sleep, and finally I saw Precop coming with his friend Anatolii. After he got inside, his eyes caught the big icon we had in our living room, the one my mother gave us. Without looking at me but keeping his eyes on the icon, he asked, "Maria, are our kids sleeping?"

"Yes, they are," I responded to him quietly.

"We must bury the icon in our yard for a while, until we come back," he said, looking at me and winking. Then he gestured with his head to Anatolii, who said, "Yes, of course, let's do it, the suggestion is good."

Anatolii helped him take it down from the wall; it was a little heavy. It took us two hours to hide it and we became tired. Anatolii left and we went to bed. I don't know how long Precop slept all those nights, but when I woke up the next day he was out already. In the afternoon, he came home running and burst into the house.

"Maria! I will take the boys to your mother's house where they will stay for a while. I will come back in a few hours for you, my love," he said, kissing me and continuing to run. I was confused and again fear gripped me instantly. After his words, I took Pauline in my arms. He came to me and held my face with both of his hands, saying, "Don't go outside, put up some food for all of us and get the clothes ready. I assure you everything is going to be okay." He kept repeating that to me and kissing me and Pauline.

The boys came to him right away; they were ready for everything. They left and I watched them from the window. I got some food, and some water and I couldn't do anything else. I started singing Pauline some lullaby songs and she fell asleep. At midnight, Precop came for me; he entered the room where I was with Pauline, got on his knees by the bed, took my hand, and kissed me. "Maria, we have to leave right now," he whispered softly to me. "You will have to take Pauline and I will take all the stuff, and also we need some warm blankets." We took everything we needed and got outside as quietly as possible. I stopped and I looked again at my house. I felt like I was leaving for an endless journey, and my soul got heavy.

Precop was going in front of me and I was behind, walking with no thoughts. "Maria just please don't be afraid; I am always here by you. Forgive me for the place where I'll take you now, I just know this is the only place where nobody will find you and your mother knows you will be there. Anatolii knows too, and you'll go there with Pauline."

He stopped and looked at me, waiting for me to say something. I said, "I am never afraid of you, for you have always been by my path in life. You make my path and I walk on it, you are my power, Precop, my man, my teacher, my husband, and my best friend. I am ready to walk in the deepest darkness, through hell, provided I will find you there, because I love you, and I know you will do the same for me. Not even the present situation can change my love for you; I am always with you and for you!" I smiled and I put my hand gently on him so he could move forward without feeling sad or bad about his decisions.

We walked quietly till we got to the cemetery, where there was a crypt of his relatives. He moved a large stone from the entrance and told me, "Go inside." I got inside, unsure where to step because it was dark. He lit some candles with the matches he had in his pocket, and afterward, he dragged the stone back to close the entrance. I was looking around, and there were three coffins. He looked at me and saw me a little scared of the place. He put all the stuff on the floor and made a bed from blankets, then he took Pauline from my arms and put her to sleep. Then he took my hand and said, "Maria, here are my grandparents and my father. Don't be scared of them; they were very nice people when they were alive, and I am sure if they were still alive, they would be happy to see how wonderful my family is."

He kept trying to make me relax and said, "Maria, you know they're getting along with some people from our village; they're buying them with a little grain and some empty words, and they get the names they need, information, who has what and what they have, who they have to start with first and who has more. And today I saw how Gavril, the alcoholic who was working at our mill, you remember? How he never showed up at work, but I was always forgiving him, letting him continue working for us in order to feed his family, paying him his salary regularly. Can you imagine they turned him into a soldier because he pointed to me and my family. After so many years, he feels the power now; he showed his face and his heart was full of hate and envy toward me. I didn't do anything bad to him. His life is a big mess now, however, I am not worried about our lands and farms or mill, I am only worried about you and our family. Unfortunately, they're shooting at people so easily and they have filled heads like our Gavril's full of hate; they don't think before hurting somebody."

Precop let go of my hand and said, "Maria, I have to leave for an hour or two. I promise I will come back before sunrise. Try to get yourself some sleep."

I laid down quietly and softly beside Pauline, and Precop put another blanket over us so we could feel warm. He went out and dragged the stone closed after him. Before sunrise, he came back, like he promised. I jumped right into his arms and hugged him. He was upset, and he brought some more bread and water for me.

"I beat Gavril because he threatened me, and I left him alive just for the sake of his wife and kids," he said, full of anger. But in a few minutes, he calmed down and said, "Maria, we will leave very soon; we just need to find a good time and good way so the soldiers will not catch us. We'll visit our mothers and boys. Georgii wants to beat everybody who is against us and he equally wants to go with me. I told him that he will go but I need some time in order to take him; for now he has to stay and protect his grandmothers." Precop paused and smiled. "I told them to stay quiet and keep our plans secret. Jacob wants to be with you, he's asking about you, but I explained everything to them and told them to get ready, that very soon we will have a long trip. I hid some more food underground for our mothers, so the soldiers will not take it from them. I hid it in the forest, not by our home, so nobody could find it and I told them the location. The soldiers are taking everything and looking everywhere."

I was listening to him, and after a while he fell asleep. In the evening, Precop was waiting for it to get dark outside so he could go out again. He kissed me and Pauline, saying, "Maria, I will come back soon as I can. Don't worry about me. And can I ask you something?" He looked at Pauline, who was in my arms, and said, "Always sing for her the same lullaby, over and over, don't change the song. I want her to remember this song!" He smiled at her and again kissed her and me and said, "I will come back."

He left again, dragging the stone after him but leaving some space for air, and I started to sing the lullaby for Pauline, and I prayed for him, so he would not be caught. He knew all the ways to hide in our village, all the trees, and all the rocks, but it was hard for him to figure out what was going on because some people from our village had joined the soldiers; they were molesting and arresting people because they knew the village layout as well as Precop knew it. Before sunrise, Precop came and I was waiting for him. He was sad, as each visit home made him sadder at the things he saw. I couldn't do anything about it, but just listened and felt sorry for people. That night he came, dragged the stone open and shut, and he drank some water without saying anything. He was tired and leaned against the wall, put his hands to his head, and sat down.

"Maria, they have made such a huge mess of our people, it is impossible to believe. Do you know Seraphima and Dimitryy? They were living down the street with five kids and right away the soldiers took their cow today, which was the only source of food for them to feed their kids. Before, when you walked through our streets, you could smell fresh bread almost at each house, and hear how people sang, laughed, and kids played. But Maria, the story has changed; everywhere now smells of blood, and at every house you hear women and kids crying. The soldiers are there day and night, everywhere inflicting pain on the people. Worse still, the villagers who are in full support of the soldiers were even given uniforms, so you can't ask or talk to anybody."

He was telling me this with so much disappointment. He fell asleep. The next night again he left and said, "Everything is going to be okay." I started singing the lullaby after praying for him. Pauline fell asleep, but I was waiting for him. I couldn't sleep, and this time I was worried about him like never before. Finally, I saw how he was dragging the stone away and he came in, bringing with him apples, pears, and grapes, all of those from our garden, and all fruits that were juicy, delicious, and cold already. The grapes were in a separate bag and very sweet like honey. He took the bunch so carefully from the bag with both hands and handed it to me, and we started eating. The grapes seemed so tasty to me.

"Maria, my love, I want to explain to you one important thing, but please, try to understand and hear it like my wife, and the strong woman you are, not like a coward," he said to me. After a short moment of silence, looking into my eyes, he smiled and started to feed me a grape; I guess I was too serious. "You know, anything can happen. When we do try to run from here, we hope everything is going to be okay, but things sometimes can turn against us." He stopped and put the grapes by the side, and after he held my face with both his hands again, he said, "Don't be scared of anything; you are strong, especially if you keep this strong power in your eyes, inside of your heart, and inside of your mind, people will feel that, and they will slow down any attack of you." He didn't know how to tell me this; he took his hands from my face and continued, "Today, the soldiers caught me by our house. I ran inside the house and right away I jumped through the back window. Once they got inside the room, they fired a shot into our closet, thinking I was still there."

He made a small pause and looked at my reaction. I was mad and scared about the whole scenario, but I tried to not show him my feelings, but my face got pale.

He took a deep breath and continued, "I just watched from outside through the window how their faces were scared about what they had done, but the main thing is that they shoot and then think. I am telling you because I just want to explain to you how indifferent they are to people; they shoot and then think," he repeated to me. "Maria, I want to tell you, if they catch us, don't run, act like we're just playing a game and nothing else. Let them feel the power, let them feel that they win, because your life is nothing against their ego, even if they know you." I was listening to him very carefully; I couldn't say anything. He fell asleep and I lay by him till Pauline woke up.

The next evening, I didn't want him to leave, I was feeling very bad. He was waiting for it to get dark outside like before, so I came to him, hugged him, and tried to say something to him, but a lump in my throat kept me from talking. He saw me pale and cold beside him, I was so scared.

He said, "I will bring the boys this time; unfortunately, you can't see your sisters and your mother. This is too dangerous, and with Pauline it is harder. Tomorrow, early, we will leave." He kissed me and left.

"I will pray and wait for you. I miss my boys too," I said with a soft voice behind him. Right after he left, like always, I started singing the lullaby and praying. I prayed all night nonstop, and exactly before sunrise, I heard footsteps by the entrance. Precop opened the entrance door, and the boys came inside. They brought food with them. "Mama!" Jacob said and he jumped in my arms; after him came Georgii. I was so happy; I hugged all three together in my arms and they too hugged Pauline and started playing with her immediately. We ate and drank, then Precop said in a hard voice, "Tomorrow, early in the morning before the sunrise, we will have to leave. Everybody has to sleep well, in order to get strength for the long trip." After a while, the kids fell asleep; they were tired and excited about the new place and the long trip they wanted to embark on. Precop and I couldn't sleep.

He told me, "Everything is good with our mothers and your sisters; don't worry about them, I made everything safe and easy for them. The soldiers had closed all the barns belonging to people, and they even put guards to watch over people's barns. People now are poor and hungry, and the soldiers have even found out how people hid their belongings in the ground. Now, they move with a long, sharp, iron hook looking for fresh ground. After they stick it into the ground, and when they pull out this hook, if it comes out with grain, they take this too. I buried ours in a safe place; they will not find anything because nobody knows it's there except our mothers."

Another day passed and at night Precop again left. He said to all of us to be ready at any minute to leave. We were waiting for him; we got everything ready for the emergency journey, and by four o'clock in the morning, he brought the horse with a carriage and we loaded everything and left. It was cold outside but we had coats, boots, and hats on. Everyone was worried.

I hugged all three of my kids. The time was when darkness receded, the time of morning twilight, and the carriage noise seemed to be so loud to us, but Precop was in a hurry to leave the village quickly, so we couldn't hide in another place till it was sunrise. Nobody said a word. I could only feel the breathing of my boys and feel Precop's excitement. The moment when the upper edge of the sun was shown above the horizon, we were out of the village and in front of us was a forest where we had to stop and stay all day till the upcoming night.

We could hear dogs barking and singing roosters from far away from our village. A little wind caught our fears, and here in this moment, suddenly a shot rang out. Precop immediately stopped the carriage and we saw a dozen soldiers coming out of the forest.

"Don't run, be calm, and find the strength!" Precop turned to us and said with a very low voice, "This time they win and that doesn't mean anything to all of us." He continued, "We will have a long trip, and unfortunately, this is a betrayal, and I know Gavril was acting weird for the last two days; he is just a coward. They were waiting for us."

He got out of the carriage with very slow-moving steps; the soldiers were coming closer and closer. The next thing, we saw Gavril, the one who had been working for us, and after a few more soldiers, the last one with heavy steps, we saw Anatolii, the best friend of Precop. His eyes were down and his pale face was simmering; he wore a soldier's uniform and he was walking behind everybody like he didn't want to, but he had to. Gavril was upfront with everybody with a nasty smile on his face, with hate in his eyes.

After Precop, we all got out of the carriage, and Precop took five or six steps to meet them, waiting for them without moving. My heart was beating like crazy, in one of my arms I was carrying Pauline, my right hand was around Jacob's neck and my hand was on Jacob's chest. I could feel his heartbeat, too, just the same rhythm as mine. Georgii made two steps after Precop and Precop turned for one second. "Georgii, stay there," he ordered him.

Gavril used his advantage and as soon as he approached Precop, he hit Precop in the face with all his power. Precop didn't fall or hit him back, and he didn't say anything, even when Anatolii came. Precop's eyes were full of strength and this annoyed more demons inside them. Even if he was silent, his eyes said that he was the winner and he was stronger than all of them and the situation he was in. Gavril couldn't look Precop in the eye and started to beat him until he fell to the ground, yet Precop didn't hit him back; he was afraid for his family.

Gavril looked at me and the kids and my tears started to flow freely. I couldn't feel the cold anymore, I couldn't hear anything, and it seemed even the wind stopped. The only thing I could feel was Jacob's heartbeat against my hand and my warm tears on my cold face. Georgii made one more step toward Gavril and Precop. His eyes were the same as Precop's, full of power and without any fears. Gavril looked at Georgii with so much hate. Precop stopped Georgii with his look and lightly shook his head, warning, "No!" After Georgii stopped, Gavril spat on the ground near him to annoy him, but Georgii did not give in; he obeyed his father.

"So, you know that we were waiting for you?" said Gavril with his nasty smiling face. "I got cold waiting and waiting for you, but it is worth it, after all. I finally see you in front of me, on your knees, and your look is pathetic, because all that you see now is helplessness, your children and your crying woman." After a little pause, he pointed to Georgii with his chin, "Look at how your puppy is staring at me. Oh, he wants to bite me, now!" He started laughing alone, "You made a copy of yourself, incredible!" There was so much sarcasm in his voice. Precop's eyes were just on me and our kids; he couldn't say anything. His eyes were telling us everything was going to be okay, and all these hard moments in our life surely will pass by.

Gavril grabbed Precop's neck from behind and got close to his ear, saying, "You know what you feel now? Betrayal." After a little pause, he said, "You are so perfect, you probably didn't even know how that feels; you are really a loser, you were not only caught, but betrayed." Gavril's face was pleased, satisfied, and disgusting.

"Yesterday, what we did with Anatolii," he continued to tell him right in his ear, with his dirty eyes on me, "we unearthed an icon that you and him buried by your house, very well, by the way. It took us time to get it out from the ground." And he turned his head to Anatolii for a few seconds, then he turned back to Precop. "You considered him your best friend, but now you see everything," he said and spat on his cheek. Precop could not stand it and turned to Anatolii, but he didn't say anything. Anatolii couldn't stand his look, so he put his head down.

To effect government directives on a lot of people or direct the people in the right way that the government needs, one simple way, which has been used for years already in many countries, is the invention of enemies to create fear. Usually, this strategy is most welcomed and believed by the majority of the non-enlightened, and unread population of the society such as terrorists, racists, religious bigots, and similar others.

CHAPTER 4

Nothing makes a powerful person so weak as a betrayal of a close and loved one, but its pain and weakness make for a short time of suffering. Afterward, you become stronger for your whole life. Who said that becoming strong mentally and spiritually is easy? It is not! It is such an unstoppable pain.

Precop was good and nice to Anatolii till it was convenient for him, it was enough to disagree, or have a different opinion, especially in this case of escape. Who was Anatolii? What made him do what he did? Was this part of his heart? Or did he look up from his heart and succumb to selfishness? He kept a dark monster inside for a long time and released it at the moment he thought was right. Was this part of his fear? When you become scared that way, they will catch you, and at least I will be in the right position of surviving.

What was he thinking about? Was this jealousy of not having plans on how to survive? Precop knew one important thing: in making a decision, you have to be clear and do everything with heart. Anatolii felt lonely without Precop's opinion and lost without his direction. He was afraid of the idea of changing.

How wonderful it is to have a person by your side and open up to him in all your colors. But it is so dangerous and hurtful, on the other hand, if the keys to your heart are in the wrong hand. It is very beautiful, like the Milky Way, if the keys are in the right hands.

Anatolii chose betrayal to save his physical body, but he forgot about his soul and his mind, which have more control over us. One day, after all, repentance too can end with a bullet in the head from your own hands.

Hunger, sex, addiction, and desire to be stronger, especially when you are not endowed with these qualities, mean nothing; it is just animal instinct if you can't control it, if you don't know its measure God puts into people to make them miserable and remind them sometimes that they are human. Your mind, your soul, and your true love are so big inside of you, so powerful, therefore, it is just too deep to dig for some people.

Like this it was and will be, always and all the times, hundreds of years before us and hundreds of years after us. People believe in other people, and rightly so, because sometimes you can find a person like you who is trusted and does not give up on you, a person exactly like you, who digs deep inside themself and shows others that there exists something more. And they will lift your soul, they will never let your soul be pulled down. It is a big lesson to learn. Who loves deeply, respects deeply, opens to you till the end and will never betray you. Also, if they will be betrayed by you, they will forget you as a nightmare, because it is deep and unforgettable till the last. But even if it was shallow, you can't delete it, it stays there forever. Anatolii remembered Precop till the end of his life. Precop believed in what Anatolii was not even capable of doing. That day, one of his best friends was deleted forever from his life. Precop never came back once he left.

Everything seemed empty and meaningless, and it was unclear what I felt. Gavril and other soldiers looked so stupid because they did not understand that their actions had caused untold hardship, hunger, and unhappiness, and we were all in the same leaking boat. They couldn't see any farther than their noses. After all, their children, their sisters, their mothers, and their relatives would die of starvation. They saw Precop as their enemy which should be destroyed; they did not understand that this was far from the case. Precop was smart and he saw things much farther. They didn't even understand that Precop's thoughts didn't stop on them. He only thought about what would happen next, and how he would protect his family. His eyes were only on us as my tears couldn't stop. I wanted to show him that I was strong, but my tears betrayed my weakness. His eyes were on Pauline, who was scared of everything;

Jacob and Georgii look like grown-up men, despite their ages.

"Enough!" ordered Anatolii. "Pick them up and take them where they are supposed to be." It seemed that I knew him for a hundred years, but on that day and at that moment, his voice sounded like a stranger's to us; his face, his look, and even as a person he had turned into a stranger.

Two soldiers grabbed Precop from the sides and picked him up from his knees. Another three soldiers came to me and the kids. One took Georgii and Jacob, and the other took me. I was holding Pauline so tight to my breast; I wanted to feel her breathing and her heartbeat.

They picked up Precop with these words, "Gazul Precop, you are an exploiter of working people and subject to dispossession." Precop winked at us and smiled softly; he did that so we would not be afraid of all these things that happened to us. Gavril and others were reminded in the end with their thinking about truth and injustice, as they thought at that time that what they did was right, and they destroyed the main enemy and those were the Fists.

Precop and I couldn't believe that at the same level where Gavril was, Anatolii was there too, when they went together against everything. Now he was on the other side of the game. Anatolii thought what he was doing was right, but unfortunately, he was totally wrong; something else made him do that. They were working for predators' parties and forcing people to work for robbers and idlers; their eyes and ears just saw class struggle, and revolution against the higher class, but the authorities simply wanted to take away households, farms, and lands from people so everything was in their control and nothing belonged to a particular individual.

You were scared to say a word to soldiers, even though they were people that you knew, people who grew up with you. Now they were executioners who had the right to shoot you. There was no time for justice; it was just survival of the fittest at that time, because at that time, people were killed without the killers being held accountable.

Life brings surprises, good and bad, and you are never prepared. And this life is so beautiful, so interesting, and unpredictable. Every day you wait for who will knock on your door, and what they will take when they leave your house. It doesn't matter whether you are rich or poor, good or bad. Usually, what they bring or take is very expensive, and as a rule, it must not be money.

This fall seemed so sad and empty, for the first time in my life. Before fall, I was overcome with happiness; we were picking the rewards of our harvest, from our lands, after hard work, but now they took everything from us, and sent us to Siberia, to a place unfamiliar to us, forcibly and unfortunately. And we did not escape.

They let us take necessary things. Precop wrote a complete refusal of all our property and gave everything to the collective farm, and we understood that there was no way back.

After all, they collected us in wooden wagons to send us to Siberia. The way to get to Siberia was a terrible and very long nightmare. There were stops where they were collecting more people, lots of children, and it was cold, too. Worse still, there was nothing to eat on the road. People were dying of hunger and cold on the way, especially children and old people.

I remember how little kids were dying in their mother's arms. I remember a woman whose child died right in her arms, but she still held him in her arms all day, wrapped in the blanket till the next stop. She didn't even want to give up the child; she was waiting to die after him and with him in her arms. Each family at that time had four to five children, the minimum however was three kids. When the wagons stopped to get more people, at the same time, soldiers were checking for the dead, and pulling them out. It was unbearable to look at all of this, how they were taking out dead children, how women were screaming, their hearts dissolving in pain because they couldn't do anything except just stay by their kids.

It was the real darkness of hell for all of us. I think even the devil himself prayed with us. All the way, I held my kids by myself, praying to God all my way there. To Siberia we were having to sleep with women and kids crying, listening to sad stories of each family; some of them burned their own houses and barns with their harvests, and even killed their animals, cows, sheep, horses, and others. They just killed them so they wouldn't have to give them away, and some of them even let the animals go into the forest.

Big and sad stories of people were told and retold amongst us in those wooden wagons, and it took a few weeks to get to Siberia. Many tears were shed during that fall, but this was nothing compared to what was ahead of us.

Finally, after all these crazy things, we got there, but nothing good was waiting for us. They unloaded us right in the forest, and all around there were swamps. They unloaded us saying, "If you think you are smart enough, show your wits and skills here."

We were not so far from the barracks where we were supposed to live but those barracks were little adapted for living. We witnessed a high mortality rate from cold, hunger, and disease. You were scared of your children sleeping because there were chances that they would never wake up again.

After we got out of the wagons, I was so happy that all my kids were alive. Everybody moved to their barracks, but the inside looked like a place for animals, with no heating, and no wood on the floor. Instead of a bed, a few boards were placed on top of each other. There was a thickening cold inside the barracks. Food was given in portions and was not enough for everyone.

"Try to sit next to each other so that they will keep you warm. I will go and bring some more branches so we will make some fire. I will fix the floor," said Precop to us when we got inside that barracks. "I had a small knife in my pocket and I made a hole in the wagon and looked on the road. We will run away from here, but not now; now will be a little hard for us since it is a long way to get to the first city."

Georgii and Jacob didn't complain about anything; they were just listening to him and they were tired and feeling sleepy. Pauline was sleeping already, after that long and cold way. Everybody was tired.

Precop said, "Everything is going to be okay, we only need time and patience. We all know what we are going through and what we will go through later. Maria, you're my wife, and you are a strong woman and mother. Georgii and Jacob, my boys, you have to listen to each other and protect your mother and your sister when I am not around." Precop patted their heads and hugged them both at the same time. "Look at Pauline, she is so little and she is going through all of this with us," he said, coming closer to her. He stroked her hair as she was sleeping wrapped in three blankets, and he kissed her. "She endures everything while we are next to her," he continued.

The boys felt more power after these words. "I will help you father, I will bring branches with you, to fix the floor," Georgii said.

"Not this time Georgii, it is dark already, hungry animals are out there, and so I will go alone. I have to check some other things. Now, get everybody by Pauline and try to sleep. Tomorrow will be a long heavy day!"

Georgii didn't insist, Jacob already had heavy eyes. Pauline and Georgii got next to him and I covered them with one more blanket.

A man or a woman has to be driven by the deep care of their family; that is one way to get superpower. Precop knew that and he put it in us, too, so we could keep fighting for ourselves and for our loved ones. When you think only about yourself, at some point, you may give up, but if you fight for those that believe in you and pray for you to be stronger so you can protect them, you get more power from within. Imagine you are to choose between God and a person you truly love. You will pick a person that you truly love. Because God is in you, in that moment, you will fight for Love till the end, not for God. You are God's hand on them, without realizing this.

Precop said, "Maria, stay here with the kids, don't go anywhere. Look at this broken door, any animal can get inside. I don't think they will go close, or get inside, but you never know. Please, stay here. I want to fix this place because I don't know how long we will be here, but for the whole winter for sure, we will have to stay here."

Veronica Braila

I went inside after him and he stopped by the door. "Listen, Maria, kids and women are crying daily, animals in the forest are not even heard, they themselves are probably afraid of our pain. It is very sad, but in all this hell we must survive, my love," Precop said to me with a soft voice. He kissed me and said, "I will come back. Stay inside with kids, stay warm, and try not to get sick; it is very important now to not get sick." He hugged me, kissed my forehead, and left.

After a while, he came back with some branches and started making the floor for us at night. I always admired Precop, admired his strong mind, his strength to never give up and to share this power and energy with us. I admired his steps ahead of everyone, and his disciplined willpower. I had never argued with him because I knew he would do everything in his power for us. So, I found a corner in this small room and hugged my knees, watching how he was fixing this little barracks. After he made a fireplace in the corner, he fixed the roof and the floor. And before morning everything was done. All night I was waiting to snuggle up to him. That night, he didn't sleep at all. The next day, he cut a big log of a tree in half and made beds for us.

We all had to work at lumbering; men, women, and older children were helping us. The other children were staying in some shed all day. There were no teachers, not even doctors, and they were staying there alone for the whole day. There were just a couple of commandants who guarded all of us. It was impossible to run; you just didn't know what side of taiga - the thick forest bordered by swamps you were on, and there were a lot of swamps.

In the evening, they gave us our children and we again went to our barracks.

On the second night, everybody was tired of working. Georgii was helping me. Jacob and Pauline had spent all day in that shed together with all the other kids.

Precop started the fireplace for us so we would be warm inside. "I talked to the commandant," said Precop to me, while putting some more wood on the fire.

"About what?" I interrupted him curiously.

"It was about you. Henceforth, you will work in the kitchen, Maria," he said to me looking at the fire.

"But how did he agree, since he doesn't know you?" I asked him.

"I gave him all of the dry prunes with nuts that we brought for us," he said with sadness in his voice.

"But Precop, that was for us, for our kids, in case there is no food!" I said a little angry with him.

"Maria, I know I barely persuaded him. I am happy that he agreed," said Precop to me. Then he turned to me and hugged me. "Maria, you will stay in this warm place and you will see our kids during the day. I just want my family to survive because now there is no exit for all of us." After a few minutes, he continued, "I was watching you working in the cold, from far away. Your hands were red from freezing when you pulled them out of your mittens and wiped your face. I watched how you lifted those heavy logs all day long. Georgii was helping you, but it was too hard for you both. Now Georgii will help you in the kitchen. I couldn't think about anything during the day, just about yours and Georgii's freezing hands and your heavy work."

Precop was right. I was working in the kitchen and always could see my kids and watch others also. I could hide some potato peels for us. I was peeling the potatoes and acted like I was throwing away the peels, but instead I was bringing them to my family to eat some extra in the evening, we were washing them and then boiling, not frying them, so the smell would not spread around. We could stay a little fuller than others and at the same time have more power to think and move forward on the next day. Precop also was bringing snails from the woods and we boiled them, too.

We stayed like this till the end of April 1931. The year was a very hard time for all of us; both the old and the young were dying almost every day. Nevertheless, we tried to survive every day. In April, snow started melting on and around those barracks where we were living, and more and more water started flooding inside. People were complaining, but the commandants were rude to all of us. Some other commissioners were there to check how we were living and they were shocked at what they saw, but for some reason, we never got any help, least of all doctors for checking the kids and some extra food.

Children started developing some flu sickness, starting with a high fever, and then they would die. This sickness was highly infectious and kids were susceptible to transferring it to each other easily, so they tried to separate them but we couldn't control or stop that ailment.

In the evening, like always, we came to our barracks. I said, "Precop, we can't stay here anymore. Please, we have to do something. Children get sick more and more here, and the commandants don't care!" At night, women were screaming from soul pain and it was so agonizing to hear all of this.

Precop was watching the fire. "Maria, I know, I was thinking to run away from here later in summer, because it is a very hard and long way to get out from taiga!" he said to me and looked at me.

I broke down and started crying. "I understand, Precop, but please do something. I don't want to experience the pain of a dying child. I am scared of that and I think this is the worst thing that can happen to a woman. I could not take this; I will go crazy," I insisted amidst tears. For the first time in my life, I raised my voice to him and felt so disappointed. "You know what happened today? Do you want to know? A woman was begging to give her sick daughter to her, that was on the verge of dying, so her child could die in her very own arms and she could probably give her a last hug, a last kiss. She just wanted to take her fear in before death, but they denied the woman this humble plea. The woman just died next to the door and her daughter died inside. O my God, it was so much pain!" I was keeping my voice loud and my tears like a river. Precop was looking at the fire, he put his clenched fists on his hips, and in a few minutes I came down and snuggled up to him. "I am scared Precop," I said.

He hugged me and kissed me. "Maria, you will not feel this pain; I will not let this happen to you," he said to me, and I believed him like always, but I was so scared for my kids. I didn't care about my life at this time, just my kids. I turned my head to them and they were sleeping so tight and so sweet like angels.

"Precop, I will die after them; I don't need my life without my kids," I continued.

"Maria, never say that and never give up. Keep your mind under control, don't let this get to you, letting your mind destroy you inside. You are my woman and these are my children. My family is strong and nothing can get them." Precop held my face in his palms and kissed me and continued, "Don't think even for a second that something can happen to you or our kids so that won't make me upset. Maria, we will leave tomorrow in the evening. Keep our kids separate, let them help you, and stay by you."

I was looking at him as he got back to the fire and the light from the fire was on his eyes and face. He put some wood on the fire to rekindle the flames. "Precop you have a plan? Where will we go? There's just forest and mud, snow and nothing else around us. Oh, are you sure we will leave tomorrow?" I was so nervous.

"Maria, now we need to go to sleep; there is no point in poisoning your soul more. Tomorrow we will have to prepare all the things we need, also try to get some more potato peels, matches, salt and water and you have to hide them. I will see what I can take from my work. I will take a knife and rope. I know the way where we have to go; we will go to the nearest city. It won't be easy to get there and it is a long way too, but we must start off."

I went and lay beside the kids. Precop was watching the fire. I was looking at him and started to think and admire him, how he could see things ahead and find solutions to any problem, and I trusted him always.

At sunrise, we all got to work. All day I tried to keep our kids around me, giving them work, to sweep the floor, fetch firewood for cooking, and keep the fire going to warm the place. I was doing everything that Precop told me to do. I hid the potato peels, salt, and matches not so far away in the forest in a scarf. We waited for Precop all day, but he couldn't come to say anything to me; he was under watch all day.

In the evening, we all came to our barracks. Precop came last, like always. "Put them to sleep Maria. Is everything ready? Were you able to do what I asked you?" he asked me. "Yes, everything is ready." I told him where the items were buried.

Veronica Braila

"I will go straight away, and bring them here from where you hid them, so the animals will not find them," he said. In five minutes, he came back with my scarf and all those hidden things. "We will hit the road tomorrow morning, earlier than sunrise." Precop lay beside me and the kids and we fell asleep.

CHAPTER 5

"Maria, Maria," Precop whispered to me in the morning. "Let's take the kids and go, my love, wrap them very well." We woke them up and hit the forest.

We were walking day and night, and Pauline was quiet. In fact, we were blessed with kids who possessed endless patience. We all kissed Pauline and got more power from her sweet cheeks. Precop told us life stories about his people all day long from his books. He was keeping our minds busy, and all the stories were extremely interesting. At night, we looked for a place to spend the night, make a fire, eat, and sleep. I and Precop were sleeping by turns because we had to watch the fire and watch for invasive, even harmful animals that could hurt the kids. Precop caught a rabbit and cooked it and we all ate and kept going.

We walked for about three weeks; we got so tired, hungry, and dirty. In fact, we barely talked to each other and it was getting dark; we could only see light from far away. Precop said, "This is the Forestier house." In about thirty minutes, we were in this house.

"Master! Master!" Precop called out to the owner of this house. A little girl of about seven years old looked out the window, then one more boy's head appeared, about five years old. And a man came out of the house. "Good evening, Master, sorry for bothering you and your family, at this time, but I need some help," said Precop. The man looked at us, and at our kids; we were dirty, my hem was full of mud, we felt ashamed for all this situation, but we were so hungry and tired, and our kids too.

"Come inside," said the man. We all went inside as he offered us and we all sat down. The chairs were clearly made by the homeowner and he was a wood master craftsman, making beautiful patterns on tables and chairs. His wife took their kids to go to sleep. They were staring at us, how dirty we were looking, so she felt we would be better if she took them to bed.

"So, what brought you guys here?" the man started the conversation.

"Master, we need a roof for a night or two, and also if you have some extra food for our kids; they are hungry, at least a piece of bread. We're trying to get to the city," Precop explained to him.

The man looked at Georgii and said, "Your kids are so disciplined; I am impressed. I have been watching your older boy in the corner by the window. In the window, my wife put some fresh cookies to cool off. Your boy looked at them for a while, and for sure he could smell them, but he took my hat from the hanger and covered them and made a few steps back, close to the door, so he would not smell those delicious fresh cookies," the man said, smiling. "That was impressive! He didn't steal them, also he didn't ask if he could take one either." Precop and I looked at Georgii and felt so proud of him. The man continued, "You can stay here for a few days, so you can wash your clothes, get enough sleep and eat." He got up, took some cookies, and shared them with us. His wife gave us some soup and she gave me some of her clothes. The man also shared some of his clothes with my husband, and they were very kind to us because they didn't have many clothes for themselves.

We were all sleeping in one room while they slept in the other. The next day, I washed our clothes with the snow water from the barrel which they usually used to keep snow after winter. The water was very soft and very good for washing clothes. We stayed there for two days, till our clothes got dry. It was at that time we told them our story. They knew about what was going on, but still were shocked by hearing other people's stories. We told them how we were treated and what crazy things we went through. The next morning, we hit the road. We were so thankful to them.

"Let me drop you at the main road," said the man. We felt uncomfortable, but we had to accept this offer because the journey was still far and we had to walk another week or two. We all got in the cart and the man dropped us about four hours away from his house. "I have to drop you here and go back because it will be dark outside very soon and my family has to be protected, so I have to return. Just walk along the road. It is a long and hard way, but it is a shortcut. You will get to the city in a week or two," the man explained.

"Thank you for your help and big heart, Master. I wish I could give you anything as a payment for everything you did for me and my family, but I have nothing to give," said Precop to the man. "We can only pray for you and your family," he continued.

"Do not worry, thanks for praying. I hope everything on your way will be easy and you will get to your home safely!" he said and drove off.

Afterwards there was another week and a few nights of walking. We had some food on the road that the woman gave us, but when we were close to the city, we were again hungry and dirty, and then we finally got to the city. There was the noise of people going back and forth, with animals, fruits, and vegetables for sale, because there was a big fair on the outskirts of the city.

Precop stopped us before we entered the city, and with a very serious face and voice he told us, "Please, everyone listen to me attentively! Here, nobody knows us and they don't have to know where we came from and what we had to go through." He stopped and looked at Georgii, took him by both of his shoulders and continued, "No matter what happens, you are a big man already, take care of your brother and sister and keep everyone together." He moved one hand to Jacob and said, "You have one important responsibility, to your little sister; always keep your eyes on her whenever your mother asks you to take care of her." He moved his hand to my shoulder and said, "I want all of you to remember, from now on we all have a different last name, Roshko, remember Roshko." And after a deep breath, he continued, "Roshko, Georgii, Roshko, Jacob, Roshko, Pauline." He said this as he touched all of them on their heads. "We will look for food, a home, then for any work to keep food on our table." He looked at me and kissed my forehead and afterward Pauline's forehead, and then he kissed our wrists.

When we were just married, on the first day, Precop kissed me on my forehead and my wrists and said that he read it in some book - although maybe he just invented it - that kissing on the forehead, wrist, and ankle meant deep love. And he always was kissing us on the forehead and wrists.

Right after we entered the fair, Precop looked around, and in a few minutes he stopped all of us again, put his hands on the kids' chests, and made a few steps to the side of us. Without looking at me, he said, "Maria, give Pauline to Georgii, right now, please." His face was changed and lost. I always listened to him, even though sometimes he was acting weirdly. "Maria, make a few steps aside from the kids," he continued.

"Now, all of you, do remember to come to this blue house on the side of the fair every Friday." He said this repeatedly without looking at me. "It doesn't matter how long we spend here; we must be here every Friday and make sure you remember your last name is Roshko," he was repeating it like it was put on auto-repeat.

"Maria, there are a lot of soldiers and they saw me already; they're coming here. But we can't run with kids, we will make it worse. Let them take the kids; I will bring them to you," he said without even looking at me. I was shocked, I was looking at him with sheer bewilderment. "Maria, make a few more steps aside; they are coming here." He made a few steps back. "Georgii, if they ask you whether we are together, tell them no. This man asked us for food and you are lost. Jacob, don't say anything, let Georgii talk."

Afterward, the soldiers started running toward us. "Maria, turn your back and leave, my love, I love you so much. They will take the kids to the children's community, feed them, and they will take us back. We might not survive there, but please, my love, be strong, wait for me. Should you become hungry, sell the necklace I gave you and buy food," Precop said.

He turned and started running but the soldiers screamed at him to stop and others caught him, put him on the ground, and beat him mercilessly. They recognized the overalls which Precop was wearing. I didn't know what to do, *Should I take the kids? But he told me to leave them. Then, what should I do? I can't leave my kids*, and I made one quick step toward my kids, but I saw Georgii turn his back to me and Jacob too, and right after a soldier came to them, I turned my back too, acting like I didn't know them. But I couldn't move in any direction, my brain froze, my body froze, and I couldn't do anything.

The soldiers came to them and asked them with a strong voice, "Is this your father?" Georgii jumped in right away, so Jacob would not say anything. "No sir, this stranger asked for food, but I can't help him, for we lost our mother a few days already, and we were also hungry too." The soldier called a few other soldiers and asked again, "But how did you lose your mother? Who is your mother?" Georgii, without any fear in his voice, explained to them that his family had to move from one city to another but he didn't know the reason. His mother told them to wait because she had to look for work so they could eat, but she never came back. Soldiers asked them their last names and Georgii spoke quickly again, "Roshko!"

I walked a few more steps ahead, looking like I was invisible, my lips were repeating in a very low voice, "Roshko!" After slowly walking, I came to some corner building and started watching. All that happened there was terrible. Georgii had Pauline in his arms and kept touching Jacob to check if he was there by him, and at the same time, Georgii was speaking with soldiers. On the other side, Precop's jacket was all covered in blood. They dragged him to the side. Soldiers took the kids and took Precop while I was still standing like a statue.

The weather was so terribly cold and I couldn't feel anything at that moment. For the first time in my life, I felt endless emptiness. I couldn't even feel that I was crying. I took a few steps; the place where I was standing was dry and I was looking around to see where to go and what to do next. These thoughts were repeated in my mind. I went closer to the blue house where Precop told us to be every Friday and I stayed there for a while, thinking he would come.

It was already dark, so I started praying for my kids, for Precop, and then I was so mad at him, imagining he was right there in front of me. *How could you bring us into such a bad situation?* I became so mad at him and then cried again. Then I realized that he did his best for us to survive, and I asked myself, *What else could he do?* I cried again as a means of relieving myself from all the emotional traumas we had passed through. Throughout the night I was outside on some bench by this blue house, waiting, talking to myself, crying, sleeping, and gathering myself into a ball.

In the morning around six, people started to gather at the fair again. I was exhausted and tired and started walking among them like a ghost; some of them were looking at me strangely. I couldn't smile, I couldn't say good morning, I was just looking around vacantly into space and I couldn't realize what was happening to me.

I felt emptiness; I couldn't feel anything else, even the God that I always believed would never leave had left me. I was walking like a ghost in a new city, among people who did not know me. I forgot the last time I ate. I was just waiting for when I would release my soul to God while I was walking among those strangers. I don't know how long I wandered like this. In fact, in one moment, I passed out.

***

I heard a man saying, "Oh my God, she is alive!" I lightly opened my eyes, and some people were around me; I passed out again. The next thing I knew, I woke up and saw a doctor by me. "You know where you are? You are in the morgue! They brought you here yesterday. You have to eat." He gave me a piece of bread. The bread looked like it had some blood on it, but I didn't care, because already I was gripped by hunger and was eating like a ravenous lion. The man was looking at me very weirdly. "We had practice with my students and I am sorry I cut you a little bit, and after you started bleeding, I realized that you were alive. You know, dead people don't bleed," he laughed. "You scared all my students; if you could have seen their faces when you opened your eyes!" I was quiet, I couldn't talk. I was eating and my arms were shaking vigorously. I was using all my power to bring this piece of bread to my mouth.

He was looking so vilely at me, and I became so scared of him. "Tomorrow, I will come to you; you have a beautiful body," he said and made this dirty, ugly smile. He was looking at me and pestering me and acting like he was doing something. I was afraid of this man, even the bread he gave me told me that. I acted like I needed to use the restroom.

I was naked, just wrapped in a bed sheet, and I was covering my body. I asked him, "Where are my clothes?" He smiled again. "You don't need them," he said. I replied, "Okay, but when I will need them, where are they?" I was insisting and trying to play his game. "I just feel cold," I continued. "There are some clothes," he said, pointing to the corner of the room. "If there are yours or somebody else's clothes, I don't know, but just take whatever you like. Anyway, they don't need those clothes anymore," he said jokingly.

I stood up and with all my power I smiled at him and I looked at the scalpel there on the table. He saw me and we both broke off to take it, but I was the first to take it because I was closer and I stuck it in his hand. He started to scream and bleed. I took some clothes there as fast as I could and ran out. I checked my neck, the necklace from Precop wasn't there, and I had to go inside again. I demanded, "Where is my necklace? I will kill you. It means more than my life." That was my first breakthrough of anger. He looked at me and pointed to the window to a small bag. I took it and ran back outside.

At that moment, I realized that I was capable of something more. I could kill because I had to live for my children. Anger is a blazing weapon and usually it is bigger than we think.

Fear wants to leave us forever, but we are the ones who feel safe with fear. Fear wants to be released. That night, part of my fears disappeared forever.

I am not scared of the darkness of nights alone. I am not scared of strange people who act like they want to harm me. In the end, I am not scared of death. I believe that what will happen will happen, therefore, why should I let this go through my body and mind? Fear is meaningless.

Another two days walking as a ghost in the city passed again. I didn't know what to do. I was waiting for Precop and I thought, *He will come with my kids and he will ask me where I have been for so long.* But he wasn't there for me, not him, not even my children. Again, sleeping outside, and holding this necklace reminded me of dancing in our living room by the fireplace, with him.

A new day arrived; I started the lonely walk again between the rows of fruits and vegetables. People had just started to display their products on the counters. Right in front of me, a woman put on her counter a box with grapes. Big grapes fell from the box to the ground and I jumped rapidly to pick them up from the ground. I took them with so much care in both hands because I knew how hard it is to keep grapes together over the winter. They easily fall apart, so you have to be very careful and gentle with handling them. I put them in the box, helping her. I held these grapes, my hands were dirty, the grapes were so beautiful, and the sun was going through them and through my fingers. I remembered Precop's hands. I remembered his smile, his charisma, but after his image I saw darkness in my eyes and I just passed out again.

CHAPTER 6

I woke up in a very dry nice and clean room. I lay on the bed, and by the bed was this woman that I helped by picking up the grapes. She was sleeping on the chair by me. On the table a candle was burning. I was feeling warm and dry for the first time in a long time. I was watching her, looking around the room; it seemed like she was living alone. I didn't want to wake her up, it was indecent, and maybe she was tired. So many questions rushed into my head: *What I am doing here? How did I get here? Who is this woman?*

I was waiting for her to wake up, and at the same time, I wasn't making any moves, any noise, so she could have enough sleep. She didn't wake up till the morning, right before sunrise. She woke up and started smiling and looking at me and she said, "Good morning! I will warm the soup for you; you have to eat."

She got up and went to the small kitchen she had and started preparing the food for me. I couldn't say anything, I was quiet. After I sat up slowly, I felt dizzy and couldn't stand, so I sat back on the bed. "Please lay down," she said to me, watching me from the kitchen. "Give me a few minutes," she continued. I lay back in the bed, feeling uncomfortable because a stranger was taking care of me. In a few minutes, she came to me with a bowl of soup and fresh bread, and she put everything close to my bed and started feeding me because my hands were shaking. I couldn't do anything. I started to eat without saying anything, rather, I broke down in tears which flowed like a river. I took a piece of fresh bread and slowly started eating, together with my tears. She was holding the spoon for me and wiped my tears, then said with a soft voice and an understanding facial expression, "Everything will be okay, please don't cry." I looked into her eyes and said with a very low voice, "Thank you!" I didn't have any power to talk, even to explain where I was coming from, what I was doing there, only my tears could show my pain, what I felt, and what I was going through. The woman was so nice to me; she didn't ask me any explanation, and I felt good that she could understand me through my tears and didn't try to dig into my soul.

After we ate, she said to me that she had to go to work and she would come back in the afternoon; I had to lay down and sleep. I thanked her again and laid back and fell asleep right away.

In a few hours, I woke up and she wasn't home. I was thinking, *she didn't even tell me her name, and she is so nice to me.* I understand that was God's hand to me when I saw the icon in the corner of her room. Whatever religion she practiced didn't matter, what mattered was her firm belief in God, plus compassion for people, and trust for total strangers; all that made her different from others.

This day, I felt I started warming up inside of me from my thoughts about how nice she was to me. I started hearing my heart, feeling my body, feeling that I kept being alive. I started praying and asked God for the same peace for my children and Precop. "Oh please God! I can't be with them at this moment. Send your angels to them, make smooth their ways and bring them safely to me." I started crying and eventually fell asleep again.

From then on, I was just stuck at that moment, when I lost all of them for years, without knowing and understanding that every day from that day represented only one thing to me: the hope of their return.

I never made any decisions in my life, but always Precop was telling me how strong I was and he was so proud of me, proud that I was his wife. I never felt that I was strong, especially at that moment. But I started to understand that on earth angels work for someone's happiness, and that can be any person; you just need to be careful. Don't make a mistake, give them the right time to show you who they are.

Veronica Braila

Some people are like candles and get burned over the night. And some people are like the sun; after the long darkness of night, they bring you endless light. Humans' destiny is to be a sun in somebody's life. But a lot of people choose to be candles for one night, which is easy and does not need any effort. Being the sun is a big power of giving, loving things, just like you would give to yourself. And angels are not visible because of the clouds in your life. But then they appear and they are humans, so don't look for wings; their wings are their deeds.

That afternoon, somebody opened the door and it was the lady who took care of me, to check on me. Immediately she looked at me, and she smiled. "You look better! I am so happy for you. Now, I will prepare some food for us and while we eat, I think it is time for us to introduce ourselves, right?" She said this with such a sweet and happy voice. I smiled back at her and got up, still feeling weak, but so much better than yesterday. I got to the kitchen and I hugged her, and she gently hugged me back. "Sorry and thank you very much for everything you did for me!" I said to her and smiled amidst my tears.

"Let's eat. I bought some delicious cookies for us, my favorite. I hope they will become your favorite too. My name is Vera." She took the plates from the cabinet and put them on the table and took two cups for tea with dessert. She was waiting for me to tell her everything that happened, and who I was, what I was doing there, but she was afraid to ask me. She was an educated person; she was only looking at me smiling and waiting. We sat down.

"I am Maria," I said.

"Nice to meet you, Maria," she responded to me and kept looking into my eyes.

"I lost my family and I am new to this city," I added and put my head down.

"Would you want to stay here and work with me?" she asked.

"Vera, yes, I do want to stay here and work. I will work hard every day, it doesn't matter how hard; this is one of the best offers that I have ever dreamed about and I am so excited. I cannot leave this city!" I told her and looked into her eyes, thinking for a moment, *Should I tell her what happened?* I felt bad because I couldn't tell her everything. I didn't know her. Plus, this story with Anatolii affected me negatively because of his betrayal of Precop. I became so scared of trusting anyone. But I was wrong. A thought rang a bell in my ears because in the same vein, *I am a stranger to her, too, and she opened her house for me, fed me, helped me, and till now she doesn't really know who I am and what I am doing here in this city.* I couldn't tell her; fear of trusting was bigger than me. I choose to not trust and not open my soul. I just started eating and looking at my plate. I wanted to be honest with her and tell her everything because I was tired of holding this pain inside of me alone. I was scared. She didn't ask me anything else, she was just reading my eyes, and she switched our conversation.

"Maria, I saw that day how you lifted the grapes from the ground with so much care, holding them with all your fingers, and very gently putting them in the box. I can tell you did something like this before." She stopped for a moment, waiting for me to say anything, but I didn't. "This is what I am doing, drying fruits like apricots, plums, raisins, make smoked plums with nuts inside, walnuts, dried apples, fresh apples, grapes, and selling them during the winter and spring."

I just was shocked by what I heard because that was what we were doing too, but we had a big amount of everything, also flour, and wheat. At that moment, my mind flew back to the past and I remembered our big mill, people were coming, leaving, and staying in line waiting for turns to make flour.

"Yes, I've done this before too, with my husband, with my kids," I said, smiling. "How is the situation in the city? Can you freely work for yourself?" She understood what I meant, smiled and said, "It's good in the villages." She got up and started making some tea and putting the cookies on the table.

"Maria, I lost my mother to cholera disease." She started to share her story first. "I was very young, about 16, and my friend got sick and I went to visit her without informing my mother. After I got sick, I brought this to my mother at home. I was left alive, but my mother, by taking care of me, got sick. Unfortunately, available vaccines were only for children and weren't enough for adults. This is my secret, my soft spot; I didn't share this with anyone. My mother was so beautiful, such a kind woman, she prepared me for her death, and told me about love, God, the soul, about life after death. She wasn't scared, she was smiling every time I came to her room. I thought she was acting like this so I would not feel guilty for the rest of my life that I did that to her. I was so stupid. She had told me to not go, but I didn't listen to her. She died. I grew up in one day, on the day when my mother passed away. You know, she told me that life after death exists and no matter how we strive for a new change, our soul is old. Who doesn't believe or feel this truth, will believe and feel it before death."

I stood up from the other side of the table and got on my knees and hugged her. I put my head in her lap. We both were lost souls and both stuck in time when you live only moment by moment.

The worst thing that humans do to themselves is stick with a past moment and wait for the same moment to repeat to fix it in a better way. But we have to realize that time is not rewinding, we must just keep going, keep living, keep loving, keep trusting, keep enjoying the feelings, keep enjoying people, and nature, and so many other things. But never forget that life is a bridge, from point A, which is our birth, to point B, which is our death. It is a bridge with holes on it, a bridge with left and right hurdles, but it is easy to lie on. The right hurdle is a beautiful thing, but it is hard to lie on. The left hurdle has the same words as the right hurdle but has different meanings.

I will tell her everything, I decided, because nothing brings you closer to another person than opening your heart to them. We were soul-mated. We spoke all night, laughing, crying, staying quiet, and starting all over with different life experiences that happened to us. I found a treasure, an amazing woman with such a big, damaged heart.

The next morning, she took me with her to the fair which was right by her home. We took all the boxes, arranged them on the counter, and started selling with smiles and a better mood, after a long night of opening up our hearts. We both needed healing. Vera was a person who would understand the past situation. She had kept her story over the years, and last night was just an open dark box full of pain. My story was fresh, filled with everyday hope, but Vera had to close all this pain and dig deep in her soul and she opened it some time, cried, and closed it back again. She kept living and smiling like everything was alright; she was a very strong woman. All this pain didn't break her. Being alone wasn't a problem or a scary thing for her, it was a decision she'd made. I thought, *How one can have such a balanced mind, be such a beautiful person, and still be alone.* She had friends, was helping others, and helping the church, but at the same time, she was lonely.

Loneliness is good, it is not bothering you, is not teasing you, and is not causing pain. It just leaves you in peace. At the same time, loneliness is very dangerous because the more you're lonely, the more you're dragged into it.

We both lived and smiled, not showing that we had brokenness inside. The only thing I wanted to change for her was her dream. I wanted to make her dream of having a real family. She was young; we both were in our early thirties. I was telling her about love, and how beautiful it is to love. For me, Precop was an example not only of a husband, but also of a human being. With him, time just flew. He used to celebrate every holiday, every birthday, and every good moment. He always wanted the sun to set as an example of him. For me and our kids, he was the footing, the foundation, but now he was somewhere else, and I would not let my mind build a coffin from our love. *He is alive, he is just late.*

I remembered how he told the boys, when he was teaching them about reading, and riding horses, any heavy work, "If it is difficult, if it is hard, that doesn't mean you are not capable of doing it, it is just time for you to change. And sometimes when it is hard and you want to keep going, remember it's always only halfway."

When we came to the fair in the morning all the people were smiling and saying, "Hi!" to us. I felt I was in a different world, where everything around us was so warm. Vera was the "sun" person and all this cold spring weather felt different than a few days ago.

Everybody had their own counter place for selling. From Vera's place I could see the blue house and I watched it all day long. Every time I saw somebody stop for a few minutes around this house, my heart was jumping with worries. So I was always checking. *Maybe somebody is waiting for me, Georgii, Jacob, my little Pauline, and the love of my life, Precop.* People moved back and forth in and around the blue house, but I didn't know any of them; all I saw were strangers.

The sun did not rise for me without my prayers for them. My life was shattered, and my mind caressed them every day. *"Oh God, give me back my family. Heaven, you seem to be so high, and all my screaming to you is lost somewhere and seems like it never reaches you. But I'll not be the one who will give up, even if you take my mind. I will still ask you till my last breath."* And I meant all these words till my last bones.

CHAPTER 7

I had long been searching for my kids everywhere, asking all the children in the community. Vera was helping me, but there was no luck. A lot of shabby children were scattered all over different cities, but without properly registering them, there was no information about them. But I never lost hope. I was working, praying, and waiting by the blue house. My mind was just pulling them, drawing them to me, I couldn't think about anything else.

Five years flew like five days. Nobody came to this blue house and my power of devotion to my family had not left me for a single second in all those years. It was late fall, conspicuous in my view were colorful trees and the shiny sun. And during another morning at the fair, I was fixing all the fruits on the counter when Vera ran in my direction with so much happiness on her face. I was watching her from far away, her face was already telling me there was good news, and my heart froze for a moment. "Maria, you know the blue house is for sale? You can buy it now, don't lose the chance. I just spoke with the lady that is selling it," she said so excitedly to me. I was so happy I jumped for joy and looked around but didn't know what to do at the moment. *Should I go now and see the house? Is she waiting for me?* These were the unanswered questions that dropped into my mind.

I was saving money to buy a small house in this city, and I was so lucky an opportunity just called, I couldn't believe it. *I will buy exactly the blue one, which was already the place where we were all supposed to meet.* "Let's go Maria, she is waiting. Should you need some more money, I will lend it to you. This house is meant to be yours," Vera said, hugging me. Vera was a person who would be honestly happy for you, and she asked another of her friends to look after the counter. We ran there and gave the woman her money. This blue house was mine, and I felt so good, like I'd found the most beautiful treasure.

I went inside and it was a nice house; there were two rooms and a kitchen, I only had to paint. On the same day in the evening, Vera went with me and we bought the paint. The next day, we worked all day painting the house. I also refreshed the color on the outside. I couldn't change the blue color and didn't want to, and this was purposely to keep the original color. Also, I refreshed the color of the bench outside, which was not so far from the color of the house, too.

My house was a little house with small windows, a small kitchen, and small rooms, but the good news was that it was mine. I was so happy I couldn't believe it, telling myself, *Now I will wait for them here.* "They will come; it is time for them to come. This is a sign," I said aloud, kneeling so tired in one of the rooms.

"Maria let's go! We have to eat and sleep. I think we did a very good job today!" Vera smiled at me.

"Vera, please, go! I will join you later."

She looked at me and said, "Maria, I will wait for you. Don't stay too much longer here now. You will have a lot of happiness here, remember my words." Then she touched my head and asked me, "What's the worst fear for you, Maria?"

I looked at her, then I got up from my knees and went to the kitchen, and from my kitchen window I could see everything, the bench where I slept my first night in this city. My feelings rolled over me, my tears flowed out. Five years is nothing; I felt like it all happened just yesterday.

"I fear the devastation of the soul because this is the devil." Vera took a deep breath, made a thoughtful face, then left.

I stayed quiet for about two hours without moving, just looking out the window; it was already dark outside. I remembered that Vera was waiting for me and I left. I closed the door but I felt that I didn't want to leave this house. In fact, I felt so tied to the place.

Veronica Braila

I came home to Vera and I told her that I couldn't stay with her any longer because I had to move. The next day, she helped me arrange everything and we stayed there in my blue house, talking all night. I told her about Georgii's temperament, how soft and gentle Jacob's temperament was, and how beautiful was my Pauline. And I told her how Precop always was telling me not to let my mind damage my soul, because sometimes things are different in our minds than in real life. We both imagined how they would look now, Precop, Georgii, Jacob and Pauline, and how we would meet them, imagining that all four of them were already together and waiting on the bench by my house. Vera was going through all this with me. I fell asleep with all this in my imagination, how I would meet them, and hug them, how Precop used to tell them stories before going to bed, and read their books, even though now they were big. Now, Precop would have new stories to tell; maybe they did, too. *What about our story? How is it going to end?* I was asking myself. Somewhere deep inside of me, I truly believed that day would come again, and I knew that I would see and hug them again.

Here came another day, the same shiny sun, the same day full of hope, full of beliefs and prayers. A year flew from the time I bought this house, a year of searching and asking about my story. All my good friends were involved, searching and asking with me for six years. I had made very honest and good friends by this time. This city felt like my city, like I already knew everything and everybody there. Time dragged very slowly from the beginning, then I got used to the idea of waiting forever.

We started taking everything from the counter, as that was the end of the day and we were laughing and talking. For Vera, I left all the products we had together in the cellar and headed home after a long day's work. In a moment, my soul moved, and my heart was beating so fast. I saw a young man seated on the bench by my home. Usually, a lot of people used to sit there, so I was already used to seeing somebody there, but today, I felt a deep shaking inside. In the beginning, I talked to everyone who was seated on this bench, but this time was different. He was a young man; he sat on this bench with his arms placed gently on his knees. He was holding his head and looking down, his hair was shaggy, and obviously he'd had no haircut for a while. The clothes on him were torn but clean.

Very slowly, I came close to him; I didn't know what to do next and how to start a conversation. *How can I see his face? Does he sleep like this? Is he sleeping? Should I ask him something?* I was getting closer to him while my heartbeat like crazy and my legs and arms were shaking uncontrollably. I stopped right in front of him. He wasn't sleeping, he was shy by the way he looked, and embarrassed. He saw my shoes and raised his head and looked for a moment.

"Mom," he said with a very confident, soft voice. He lightly smiled as tears rolled out freely. I got cold in one second, shocked like an electric current ran all over my body. This grown man was my oldest son, Georgii! I fell to my knees and hugged him. I thought I was going crazy. I was screaming and crying at the same time. I kissed and hugged him with the loving tenderness of a mother. I couldn't believe my son Georgii was in front of me.

In a few minutes, Vera was by me saying, "Get in the house, Maria!" She started grabbing us and lightly pushing us to go inside our home because we attracted too much attention, which was still dangerous at that time. We calmed down a little.

"Let's go home," I told him and pointed to the blue house. He looked at me and again said, "Mom." We couldn't release each other. We got inside the home.

"Mom, who does this house belongs to?" he asked me, surprised.

"It's mine, I bought it a year ago."

· He looked like he hadn't eaten for a while, so I started preparing some food for him. He sat on the chair in the kitchen and looked around. I put some soup and fresh bread in front of him and I couldn't take my eyes away from him. He was eighteen years old. I decided to give him space to eat before I asked where he had been. He was very hungry and so skinny; only bones were visible and the chaotic hair on his head. He started eating fast, then realized that I was watching him, and after a quick look at me, he slowed down.

"Mom, I am sorry," he said. "I didn't eat for a few days. It took me two days of boarding the train and one day of trekking to reach here, and then I wasn't sure if it was here or not, or whether I would see anybody here or not, but this was my only dream to meet you someday. I was walking in the city, checking for work all day today." He paused, then asked, "Where is our father? Is he working? I can't wait to see him." He smiled through his tears, so much pain was coming out of him. I couldn't ask him anything yet, I was just watching and touching his head and shoulders. "Mom, did you eat? Why didn't you eat? Is there enough food for you?" he asked me, looking into my eyes with so much passion.

"Georgii, yes, there is enough food. I am working, I have money, and everything is good!" I realized that he had endured such hunger and this was why he was asking me that. *Oh my poor child!* Again, I touched his shoulder, got up, and gave him more bread and more soup.

"Mom, I know where Jacob and Pauline are. I found them a few years ago. You know, they separated us from one another, but we weren't far from each other and they settled in another city."

I was so happy I found all my kids in one day. How long I waited for this day. One day in six years, always waiting and hoping for one day, and this day finally came today. *Thank you, thank you, thank you for all my angels, God of the Universe, for bringing them to me, and I am here prepared, ready for them with everything: food, and roof.* I was looking at my Georgii with so much love and joy.

"Mom, thank you." His eyes were wet from time to time.

"Georgii, I don't know where your father is; I don't know anything about him either. I miss him, in fact, I miss all of you!"

He looked at me and said, "He will come here. I believe he is on the way, Mom." He got up from the table and hugged me. "My way was always on the way here, and his way too; he is on the way to where we are, and he will not miss it." He smiled with hope.

"Georgii, tell me everything; you went through a hard time, right? Your eyes are full of pain." I put my hand on his cheek.

"What do I tell you? It was hard, but why should I complain? Do you know how many kids are out there on the street, struggling, and hungry? Why did Stalin do that to his country? Who is this guy? Why was there no information about him, and why are people scared to say his name?"

I looked at him and said, "Georgii, my son, now is not the right time to speak about this; maybe years from now. Not so long ago, a man put his cup of tea on Stalin's picture in a magazine and some other guys just went and declared that he just was drunk. But the next day, they arrested him because the picture on the magazine was dirty from his teacup. They said that he was against Stalin and spread discord. I think we have to be quiet about politics now, because people are scared; nobody wants to deal with it. There is no justice now."

He looked disappointed and changed the conversation. "Mom, you are so brave. You bought this house?" He looked around, his eyes shone again. He felt at home; he felt protected, and he felt good.

After we ate, he took a shower. The only clothes he had were the ones he wore, and they were already torn. I was thinking of asking him more about Jacob and Pauline, and what he had gone through, but he was so exhausted that he fell asleep. There would be the opportunity for me to hear everything, and equally to know where they were.

The next morning, I couldn't wait till sunrise to go to the fair and buy him some clothes. I spoke with one of my friends who did very well at cutting hair, where I could take my son after buying some fresh bread and running home before he woke up. When I got inside, he was awake, sitting and waiting for me. "Mom," he said softly, right as I got inside. He tried not to show it, but like a kid, he couldn't take his eyes off me. And when I tried to catch his eyes, he put them down, not wanting me to see the child in his eyes. He wanted me to see a man there with me. I said, "Georgii, I bought you new clothes, I hope you will like them." He smiled and with a little breathless voice and such a beautiful smile, he said, "Mom, I like everything." I gave him the clothes and told him that the barber was waiting for him. He took my hand and kissed me. "Mom, thank you for everything that you're doing for me. It feels like paradise to me, like a nice dream. I still can't believe it, I am here with you." His eyes teared up in a sober reflection. His deep pain was coming out through his tired young man's eyes.

While he was changing his clothes, I was preparing him breakfast. He came to the kitchen and I couldn't wait to hear how Jacob and Pauline were. Again, his soft voice behind me said, "Mom." I turned to him, he was dressed up and lightly smiling. He was looking so good, even though the clothes were a little too big on him. He looked like his father. I couldn't control myself; I started crying and hugged him. I couldn't get enough of him. I took in his aroma; he smelled like when he was little. I was missing them all, and now, by looking at him, I saw everyone. I sat down and we ate. After a few minutes, he started telling me what happened to them, from day one.

"They took us on that day, brought us to some office, where there were two ladies, two men, and they asked us some questions after a lady took us and fed us. Then they took us to another city on the same day. There, they separated us into different orphanage homes; they separated us because the lady was saying Jacob and Pauline were in the category of little kids and I was older, good enough for work, so I belonged in another category of kids. There were a lot of kids crying, and a lot of brothers and sisters who lost each other on that day. I gave a promise to Jacob that day that I would find him, and I would come back after him and Pauline. I did keep my promise but it took me three years. I was looking for them, often running away from the orphanage, which was very hard, because every time I came back, they punished me."

He stopped for a moment and ate some more. "After a year, we started running away from the orphanage; most of the time, we were in the street. I made friends, so there were four of us and I was their leader, they received instructions from me. Nobody had a family, so we were like one family, sharing bread between each other. Sometimes, we were working for food, and other times, we would just starve. I'm sorry Mom, to bother you with these ugly experiences, but we didn't have anything to eat. We were like dogs in the street. When your life is that terrible, you feel so miserable. Nobody wants to look into your eyes to find your pain. Maybe you are not like this, maybe you are just hungry, and everybody is just ignoring you, hating you, and you do the same in return, ignoring them, hating, showcasing injustice, so we had to do that." He looked deep into my eyes. I was proud of him; at least he is alive and he is here, which means so much to me.

"One day, one of my friends came to me and told me that he knew one guy whose last name was Roshko, like mine. I just lost myself, I couldn't believe it. I couldn't wait to go and check who this guy was. All my friends knew I was looking for my brother and sister, and they were helping me, too. Also, he told me that the guy was beaten and was all day long begging in the street. He told me the location wasn't that far. I went there on the same day, and Mom, when I saw him…" He stopped and gulped, trying to stop his tears. "Mom, he was covered with dust. Under the fence I came to him. He didn't even raise his head, he covered his head; he thought I would beat him, without looking at me. I put my hands on his shoulders, I said, 'Jacob, it's me.' He looked at me and he started crying, his face was covered in dust, his eyes tired of suffering. I gave him my hand and I raised him from the ground. I asked him what happened, why he was like this. He told me there were some guys in the orphanage who were constantly beating him to beg in the street, and after, they would take everything. I took him and I fed him, and afterward, he told me that he knew where Pauline was and he visited her from time to time; he never lost her. He said that every time he saw her, he told her that she had family and had been missing her brothers, mother, and father. He assured Pauline that one day somebody would take her from there, or they would run away together. He also said that he was reluctant to go to her dirty and meet her, because she was different, she had a strong temper, and she would never let anybody insult her. She was very beautiful and confident, always wearing clean dresses. Some woman visited her and wanted to adopt her probably." He smiled. I couldn't interrupt him with anything, and I was very happy and listening so eagerly.

"I told Jacob that, first, we have to fix his problems," he continued, "and later he would show me where Pauline was because it looked like everything was good with her. And after we ate, and Jacob had to go back, I and my boys went after him to see what would happen. Jacob was walking slowly and his head was fixed down and he kept looking back at us. I was motioning him to keep going, we had his back, and in a few minutes four older guys came to him and asked where he had been so long, and where was the money that he made from the food he got from people, and where he got a pair of shoes. I gave him my shoes because he had very bad ones; even though mine were a little big on him, he was happy. They started pushing him. Oh my God, Mom, when we got out there, there was a big fight. We beat them up, blood was gushing out, and they were screaming that they would never touch him again!" He started laughing lightly and looked proudly at me. "Mom, I will never let anybody hurt you, now that I am with you." He touched my face like Precop did, and a flash of electric shock ran all over my body like a torrent. It had been a long time since I experienced that feeling.

He continued, "After this fight, I started seeing Jacob often and he was looking better than before. I tried to meet Pauline but it was harder than I thought. I couldn't catch her somewhere outside, I couldn't get inside either. She was busy, reading books, also she was telling Jacob that he had to read too, because books made one a smart and interesting person. He could talk about the books to people, and you become interested in the story. They were doing very well with each other. I had to leave them, without seeing Pauline, and went back to the other city because we didn't have any money and there was no work for us, so I left them. I was coming back and communicating with Jacob only; I couldn't see her for years."

He stopped with sadness on his face, then said, "I know it took so long to see her, but I just couldn't. One day, I just started following her, staying there for days and waiting. One day, I saw three beautiful girls walking together. She was the one in the middle with long beautiful hair, big beautiful blue eyes I just felt it. The girls started giggling when they saw I was looking at them, Pauline was serious and told them to stop, but one of the girls told Pauline, 'Look, this guy is looking at you.' And Pauline said, 'NO, he is looking at you. Let's go faster, he is a dirty stranger!'" He started laughing and looked at me. "Mom, I couldn't speak with her on that day, I could speak with everybody, about everything, but that day, I couldn't say a word to them; they just passed me and left."

He went on with his story, "I got back to my city and again I started to work. I bought some better clothes, cut my hair so I could look good because she said I was a dirty stranger, and all the girls started laughing at me!" He smiled and I smiled with him, too.

"In three weeks, I went back. I saw Jacob first and talked to him, and he was good, nobody bullied him again. I told him what happened between me and Pauline, and he agreed to go with me. She was with the same girls, but this time she saw me and came to me by herself and said, 'Hey, I don't like it already. I see you here a second time, now tell me what you want from us?' She was so serious, and I smiled and said, 'Pauline, it's me, Georgii, your brother.' She looked at me from my head to my toes and back with apprehension and said, 'I have to ask Jacob, I don't remember you.' 'That's okay,' said I, and she continued, 'Where are my parents?' And without knowing where you were, Mom, I promised her that one day I would bring her to you. She smiled, she has your smile. I relaxed when I saw her smile and I remembered you.

"Henceforth, I started visiting them very often. I tried my best to show them we were family. They had their own stories to tell, and I had mine too, so we were sharing with each other. Pauline always brought food and sweets each time we met. Jacob was seeing her more often than me. She chose to be very careful disclosing some information about herself to me, but Jacob was telling me everything she was telling him. Some woman was treating her as a daughter. Pauline was treating us as her brothers, sharing every piece of bread with us. Pauline's temper was so strong. Her look was like sunshine; whenever I saw her, I felt happy." He smiled and looked at me. "Mom, she looks like you and our grandmother," he repeated.

CHAPTER 8

Only the faith inside of me was warming me up on those long Siberian nights of praying by a small fireplace, where I lived with that crazy faith... that faith from which I was afraid I would just go crazy one day. It was faith full of power, and cold as a rock when you're trying to look ahead, trying to touch something, and all-around is ice without soul. I was walking and always looking behind for more footprints, but I could hear only mine. I was waiting for them. I didn't know if God existed, but I was knocking on His door with prayers every night for my family.

Now, I looked at my son's eyes. I saw the small door to my home, I heard my mother's voice, and I saw how, in the evening, with a small candle in the kitchen, I told her everything that happened to me. I saw there my children and Precop. He always winked and smiled at me every time he caught my eyes. I could see now that

Georgii was tired, thoughtful, and empty of dreams in his eyes. His fist was constantly clenched, his other hand was holding that hot tea I made for him. He knew that nobody could help us. He took all this responsibility for us at such a young age. His face was so serious, he constantly had his eyes down. I couldn't stop looking at Georgii in my mind and prayed for him thus: "God, you are with me and for me. Like a wind, bring to me that day when I can smile and dance." Every day, waiting for tomorrow, every morning and evening felt the same. I couldn't tell any difference between days and nights, but now a door was open and then I knew where my kids were.

The next day there was such a beautiful morning. After so many years, I felt different, alive; I felt the sun coming in through the window on my face, like a good dream, and I was enjoying this hot tea with my oldest son. My faith got more powerful. *Soon I will see all my kids.*

After all this, I started preparing everything that we needed for the journey. I couldn't wait to see them; my mind was there already. They were alone and separated for such a long time, and my dreams lit up again. *It does not matter how they will receive me; after so long a time, I just want to see them as soon as possible.*

"God," I prayed, "look at how I am now, ready for the big fight of faith, for any war, ready to take anything, just enough to light up a little of my way. I have everything, such as a home where to bring them, feed them… just look at me, I am so strong and so ready for them, Oh God."

We prepared food and some clothes and I took the train with Georgii to the city where Jacob and Pauline were. Georgii spoke with the lady there who already knew him, to let us board the train without documents. It was a long journey. I couldn't eat, I couldn't sleep, and I was just praying and crying all the long way. I was imagining how I would meet them, hugging them, kissing them, but also a deep feeling of fear gripped me that they were so big now. *What would they look like? How would they react when they saw me? Would they understand that I was always looking for them, or would they think that I just abandoned them?* All these thoughts continued to beg for answers, over and over again in my mind. It took us three days to get there and we were all connected through prayers to heaven. Finally, we got there.

When we arrived, there was another problem. I couldn't take them, just like that, from the orphanage; I didn't have any documents. My last name on my passport was different than the name they had registered with there. Also, I couldn't tell anyone who I was, especially that I ran away a few years earlier from Kulaks/Fists. So, in this case, we had only one option, to kidnap them, which was very dangerous because we could get caught and put in prison.

First of all, I had to meet them, without going inside and asking for them. "Mom, you have to stay outside. I will go around there and check," Georgii told me, and took me by a big oak tree that was in front of that orphanage. He knew this place very well; he used to hide by this tree every time he came to Jacob. I was so distressed; we came first to take Jacob because his escape was easier.

After a while, I lost Georgii from my sight. He went somewhere around the building and told me to stay in one place, so I couldn't go anywhere to check or to ask. After around three hours, I was worried, and my legs couldn't hold me up with all this anxiety. I sat down and leaned against the tree, and all those memories started coming back: when they were little and fighting because of bugs; when there was peace and love; when we were enjoying life; those moments from winter and summer, fall and spring; those moments Precop used to keep us always happy and healthy, feeding us with a mix of honey and nuts and sesames and fruits, different kinds of hot teas. Every day I was preparing different kinds of food; everything was so tasty and delicious, especially when you love and you are loved. Life seemed to be a paradise for all of us. My soul craved happiness and peace for such a long time.

We don't appreciate our time; time can change. It was so pleasing to have a beautiful past; when you felt bad, from time to time you just dive back into your beautiful memories. It sometimes helps you to feel better, to move on, and to fight for similar or better moments.

How ridiculous for some people who live their lives upside down, when there is such sky above us. I lightly opened my eyes and looked at the sky with this sunshine spreading around, scared of my thoughts that were telling me there can be no more time.

In a moment, I heard two boys' voices behind the tree. They were coming closer and closer to the place where I was. My heart started beating like a rabbit's. I tried to stand up but my legs did not obey me. I couldn't move, and in a moment, they just came around the tree and stood in front of me.

"Jacob," I pronounced quietly. Jacob was looking at me so deeply. He looked so tall and skinny and exhausted. I stretched out my hands to him, my tears rolled out, and he had the same reaction. They were just feelings of our innermost connectedness; we both were very sensitive inside and so connected. He was my boy, and he fell on his knees in front of me, and we hugged each other. I kissed him all over his face and smiled at him, holding his face in my palms. Georgii was looking at us with happiness. "Here is your mommy, Jacob," he said and smiled at us. Like a joke, he always used to say that to Jacob when he was little. I couldn't believe my happiness. Everything around me was moving, and I felt so happy, dizzy with happiness. "Oh God, you brought them to me, thank you!" I said, looking to the sky with light that was on my face, through the leaves of this old, big oak tree. We had some food for Jacob and us and we got hungry and we sat down.

Jacob said, "Mom, I missed you so much, our family, and our father. Where is he?" I took his hand. "I don't know where your father is, my son." He looked sad and told me, "Mom, no matter what, how hard things were for me here, I always knew you would come for us; Georgii would come, or our father. I always knew, Mom, and always told Pauline this too, I was singing for her your lullaby; even now she is asking me to do that!" Jacob's eyes were so shiny with happiness.

"Jacob where is Pauline? We have to find her too, and leave this city as soon as we can," said Georgii with seriousness in his voice. Jacob replied, "Now, she is not here, the lady that often visits her, took her somewhere. She usually brings Pauline back and she wants to adopt her, but she has some issues with documentation." And when he said this, he looked at me, and something cut me inside and I got so worried and had to breathe deeply.

"Mom," said Georgii, and put his hand on my shoulder. "This will never happen! Okay? This will never happen. Look, at us, we are all three here for her. Do you think we will let her go? Never!" I started crying because I didn't know. What if she chose not to want to go with us? Maybe this lady has become a mother to her because she was so little when we separated. "How long did this lady visit her?" I asked Jacob. He looked at Georgii, and Georgii's face didn't change; it was cold as a rock, with no reaction. "After a year since we came here, the lady found Pauline. She liked her and started visiting her, buying her gifts, taking her out, but I don't know why exactly she couldn't take her."

I became disappointed and I put my head down, and my tears started dropping on my cheeks. Georgii lifted my face under my chin and said, "The reason why this lady can't take her is the power of your prayers; that holds her and us here. She is my sister and your daughter. Do you hear me, Mom?" He raised his voice. "We are here to take her; she is ours and she is our little sunshine!"

I took my head from his hand and said, "I feel sorry for all of us, including this lady. She was loving and protecting her for so many years, and now somebody will have this forever broken heart, this pain. Maybe we should talk to her, explain things to her?" I looked at Georgii; he was standing, and he said, "Stop Mom! No! She may refuse us and make the matter worse. I will take you back and come back for her by myself. We can't stay here too long. We don't know when she will come back. We don't need this compassion for this lady; she can easily betray us, take Pauline away from us. We don't know if she will take pity on us. It's dangerous to risk our feelings." Georgii started helping us to stand up from the ground. "People already are staring at us. We don't need this attention and problems now."

We three had to leave. Georgii spoke again with the lady there to take us back. We returned home, but throughout the journey, we didn't exchange a word with each other.

When we reached my house, Jacob gazed at it with a strange look. "I remember this house. Isn't this where we were supposed to meet?" He was curiously looking around. Georgii smiled and said, "Our mom bought this house. Is that cool?" And he looked so proud of me. "Mom, how did you do this? You had no money!" I put my hand on his shoulder, "I met here a sun!" He remembered how Precop used to tell us about people being "suns" and "candles".

We all recalled him saying some people are like a sun in your life, bringing beautiful days to you every day, and others are like candles; they don't have energy, they don't have enough light for their life, never mind talking about sharing light with others, and with just one small wind, the candle is gone.

We went inside, I made some tea, and we ate, and went to bed. They were sleeping so deep and tight and I was looking at them, so happy. I couldn't believe they were here in this house with me. I couldn't get enough of them. The crackling candle seemed so loud, and they were so peaceful. I started praying for Pauline and Precop. I went to bed late, with so many thoughts and questions. *How will Georgii bring Pauline? Should I let him go back alone? Should I let Jacob go with him?* I was scared to lose both of them again.

The next morning, I woke up and Georgii was awake already. I thought nobody could wake up earlier than me and I was surprised. He made some tea and smiled at me. "Good morning, Mom, you are so beautiful this morning! We need work for me and Jacob." I smiled back at him. My soul was blooming. *He told me I am beautiful, his voice was like Precop's,* and my world stopped for a second. "Yes, you will help me with the products, to bring them to buy and sell them, to dry them. I will show you; let's go to the barn."

We went to the barn where we had all these fruits and vegetables. Afterward, we went back inside the house and finished breakfast. Both of us were looking at Jacob and felt sorry to wake him up. We stayed quiet and waited for him to wake up by himself. He woke up so happy and peaceful and we made him some fresh breakfast too. Georgii took him outside to show him the work. Vera visited us and she was very happy for me that finally I found my sons. I said that they would help us with work; we were not alone anymore, and she was happy. We left them working and went together to church. Attendance at churches at the time was still illegal, but we knew where to attend. It was such a beautiful day. My thoughts were recovering little by little, and my soul was like a puzzle; some pieces were in place, while other pieces just needed time and patience to be fixed properly.

We didn't wait too long. In one week, Georgii told us he was going for Pauline and he wanted to go alone. I couldn't say anything. I really wanted to go and Jacob was insisting on going with him, saying that Pauline won't go with him because he knew her better than Georgii. She would only follow them if Jacob was there, but Georgii insisted and promised me and Jacob that he would bring her to us. It would be more difficult and dangerous, and if we went together, we could be caught. He prepared his bag with food and a jacket. I gave him a letter to give the lady who used to visit Pauline. In this letter, I explained everything and thanked her for all she had done.

In a few days, Georgii got there. He waited for Pauline to come out for two days and two nights, sleeping on the street, and finally he caught her out with one of her friends. "Pauline," he called to her. "Come here, I need to talk to you." She looked at her friend and told her to stay there so she could talk with him apart. She came straight to him, looking straight into his eyes and not saying anything, just carefully listening to what he would say. "Pauline, it is time to go to our mother," he said with fear in his voice. Somewhere deep inside him, he was afraid that she would not go, and feeling afraid, for some reason it was hard to talk to her. Fear was taking over, and with a cold voice, she asked, "Where is Jacob? Where is my mom?" Like he was a stranger, Georgii put his head down, because there was "no" in this conversation, no connection. Then he raised his head and his voice became harder. "It's dangerous for them to be here. I have been looking for you for two days. I know you don't trust me." He paused for a moment and looked at her and hardly smiled. "You are so beautiful! Your hair and eyes are exactly like our grandmother, your face features with full lips and a gentle voice are like our mother. Your temper, to fight and lead forever, that you took from our father. I want you to go and prepare your bags, because without you I will not go anywhere. Come rain or wind, I will stay here like a dog, waiting for you to come out, but before you carry your bags, I want you to find a big mirror and look for a minute, or for an hour. Take your time. Look in this mirror. Ask who you are, and who you belong to. Your brain may not remember because you were little, but your blood that's circulating through all your body knows that you are my sister and your mom is waiting and praying for you every moment of her life, endlessly in hope and faith." He looked aside and then back to her, and after a deep breath, continued, "Our mother used to make the best soup ever. Her hugs made you feel calm and peaceful and at home, no matter where you were. She kissed your forehead and hands before you went to sleep, no matter how old you were. She is an angel. Now go and make sure nobody sees you. I will be here waiting for you. Make sure everybody is sleeping before you leave! Also, take this letter for the lady that used to visit you; it is from our mother." He handed the letter to her. Pauline took the letter and looked at him without saying a word. Her face looked thoughtful, and she turned around and left.

"Pauline, what happened? Why are you crying? What did this guy tell you?" asked her friend when she saw her face. Georgii took another deep breath because he understood that he had touched her soul and bones. She would definitely make the right decision and that was his goal because there was no time and they had to leave before anybody discovered he was looking for her there and they would be in trouble.

Pauline went into her room, sat on her bed, and opened the letter from her mother, which was addressed to the lady who was visiting her:

The pain in my soul is stronger than physical pain. From the physical pain, you endure; from the soul pain, you get scared that you will go crazy, and you pray because you are on the edge of the deepest darkness – the unknown. Your mind is playing the worst game, and in this game you are a loser, because you don't know the truth. My daughter's smell is the best smell in the world. Her eyes are more than a whole galaxy to me, and her smile gives me more promises of a better life than the sun. She is so deep in my subconsciousness that I can smell her when I dream of her. I always hoped that I would hug and kiss her again; that is what I only lived with till now. You are the angel that I asked God for her. I want to thank you! I send deep thanks to you for watching my little, gentle, and tender princess. P.S Maria, Pauline's mother.

Around 1 am, Georgii saw her getting out of a window. She threw her bag first through the window and then she jumped. She came right to him, stopped in front of him, looked into his eyes and said, "If I do not like something, I can come back anytime. The second thing, if you hurt me with something or lie to me, you will regret it a million times." Her eyes were sparkling and beautiful. Georgii laughed, then made his face mean and said, "Okay." Throughout the three days on the train, she was questioning him about everything he knew.

I was outside with two of my friends when they came. I couldn't move or say anything, I just watched them approaching me. Georgii was holding the bags and Pauline looked very relaxed and happy, laughing with him. During those three days on the train, Georgii took all her doubts and fears away from her. For a moment, she stopped and her face became more serious. She looked right at me, even though there were three of us women standing there, but she recognized me right away. She started walking slowly and scanning me, my arms, and my hair. My tears rolled out freely. I couldn't make any moves, thinking, *and right in front of me is my little, beautiful sunshine.*

I took her hand with both of my hands and kissed her. I hugged her very gently. And I was scared to not hurt her. I took her head in my hands and kissed her forehead, started touching her hair and quietly crying. This was my baby, my girl, everything stopped in this world. "Let's go home," I told them. I took her hand and Georgii followed us. I didn't know how to deal with her, she was stronger than I expected. She didn't show any emotions, she was just analyzing the situation. As soon as we got inside our home she said, "Mom, I always was waiting for you, when you would come and take me from there. I was always missing you. Every evening, I went to bed with thoughts about you; every morning, I was telling myself that this may be the day when my mom will come and take me." She hugged me tight and long.

Jacob saw her and jumped up and hugged us. Georgii hugged all three of us and said, "All your babies are here and very hungry." He smiled, and everybody started laughing. I stood up right away and started warming the soup for them and cutting bread. They were all at the table, laughing and talking. I was looking at them, so happy, and everything was like a dream. *They are so grown, such smart personalities, and I am so proud of them. So, I am not alone anymore.*

CHAPTER 9

Precop was caught for the third time running from Aleksandrovsky Central Convict Prison, one of the convict prisons of pre-revolutionary Russia. At this time, there was no escape; prisoners were taken there on order of the death penalty. There were eight of them. Precop pulled out a screw he had previously hidden in his shoe and started picking at his handcuff. "This is the last chance; there is no other chance, anyway. We're going to die, so it is better to fight till the end," said Precop to the others in the dark prison carriage. "I know where we are, we just need the right time to jump. Behind us is another carriage with five soldiers, and with us are another three. When they stop to rest, we have to use the opportunity, we have to run all different directions. Unfortunately, today is going to be the last day of living for somebody."

Veronica Braila

They were tired and dirty and hungry, with sad faces looking down and just agreeing with Precop. Everybody was sharing the idea of escaping, only one strange guy was just listening and not saying anything. "Hey, you, won't you run with us?" Precop asked him. And he raised his eyes and looked at Precop and didn't answer him. "It looks like he's not," said one of the guys from the carriage. "Leave him alone, it looks like for him it doesn't matter whether he dies today or tomorrow; probably he is already dead," said another prisoner. Precop looked at the guy for a few seconds, felt sorry for him, and looked around at everyone. "Imagine that as soon as you stop, or give up, they begin to prepare your coffin, hammer, and nails, and measure the size. As soon as you run, they stop for a break and they leave the coffin alone. If you stop, or accidentally stumble, the coffin is ready for you, my friend," said Precop. He spoke in a low voice but his words stuck in everybody's throat and eyes. He was smiling, even though it wasn't a funny situation.

Nobody moved for a few seconds. Finally, they got to the point where they stopped the carriage to take a break. By that time, everybody was free from handcuffs. Precop knew how to unlock them with that screw; it wasn't his first time. In the next moment, when the carriage stopped, they broke the door and got out into the woods, all running in different directions. Soldiers fired without any regrets, for their lives were worth nothing. The men were running with all their power, everywhere in the woods. All the animals lurched from that big noise around them; they had no power to run. Also, that silent guy who didn't want to talk in the carriage held on with all his power behind Precop.

There were shots fired, screaming, barking dogs behind, but you just keep running, with no thoughts in your mind of looking back, just the sound of broken branches underfoot, and if you felt that and still had the power to run and you didn't fall, it meant that the bullet hadn't hit your body yet.

Precop ran to the river down the hill. There were large chunks of ice along the river banks and he got into the water and dragged one on top of him. The silent guy by him did the same thing. The water was so cold, but fears and desire to live kept them warm. In about one hour, they heard one of the soldiers holler, "Let's go, just two escaped. We didn't catch them, but the wolves will eat them; there is no chance of survival!" And they left. It was so dark outside, and they got out of the water, wet, cold, hungry, tired, and they were just walking silently. There was a full moon that night. Precop raised his eyes to the sky and said, "The sky is so beautiful tonight. Look at the stars, the moon, if our life ends here, they will shine the same brightness as now." He put his head down. The silent guy looked up and asked Precop, "You believe that somewhere there is God? But for me, I don't."

"Does the existence of God matter? Believing is the magic that's changing your inner mind and releasing the present pain to something better. Believing is like medicine for your mind; in a magical way it releases and calms the hell where your body and mind are now, especially when you don't have any other choice. Doubts are hell; believing is foolish but it helps. I am not scared of God. You may say that God is for wicked people, so they believe and get stronger. But I want to see you strong enough to love the emptiness, to deal with real darkness face to face, see your child's last breath, and after this, live without God. I think people's minds haven't touched this power or strength without Him yet. In the end, nothing is bad in believing if it saves you."

Precop said, "Let's hide here in the hollow of this big tree. There are a lot of wolves here and we don't have a fire, and my matches are wet, so we have to pass the night."

Precop started praying before he went to sleep in his usual manner. "I don't believe in God," said the quiet guy to Precop. "'If someone could prove to me that there's Christ outside the truth, and indeed, it would be that the truth is outside of Christ, then I would rather stay with Christ than with the truth'- Dostoevsky." Precop quoted Dostoevsky and didn't even look at him. In the morning again they continued the journey. It was so cold and the sun was very shiny. They were eating worms and snails from the trees for their food. Approaching the night, they found a house with lights inside.

"It looks like somebody lives there; we are lucky," Precop said. They started looking around through the windows. A woman around seventy years old was there, and a boy around thirteen years old. They knocked on the door. The woman was scared to open it but she had a gun so she opened her door with the gun in her hands and very carefully. "What brought you here at night?" she asked.

"Please, let us stay for a night; we are hungry and lost. I promise that we will do nothing bad. I have family and I am going to meet them. I don't want to die until I see them, please!" The lady looked at them, two strangers at night, and said, "Go away, there is no place here to sleep. The only help I can give you is some bread!" And she called to the boy with a strong, rude voice, "Ivan bring me some bread for these two hungry dogs." Precop said, "Thank you, ma'am, God bless you. I really appreciate any help." The lady looked at him and said, "Tell me the Our Father prayer." Precop smiled and started the Our Father to her. The woman's face changed from that of a rude and cold woman to that of a woman who understood someone else's grief. She smiled warmly and said, "Come inside and tell me everything."

They stayed there all night. The lady put them to sleep on the floor. "There was no space for us," Precop said later. "We spoke for a few hours, drinking hot tea and warming ourselves by the fireplace. The lady told us her story, how she lived there with her husband and he passed away and she was there alone, till this boy came to her from nowhere. He'd lost his family, and his family was one of the Fists. She adopted him and he was helping her. The boy was very smart and educated; he listened to her and always kept an eye on us." However, Precop's mind was with his family.

The next day when Precop woke up, the lady and the boy were awake already. "I will guide you to the city; it is not too far from here and you just have to pass the river. Nevertheless, I will go with you till the river. I know these woods by heart," said Ivan. And looking at the lady, she approved his decision, so it seemed like they had already talked about it earlier in the morning. They could understand each other in half a word. Precop was very thankful and very happy about their help. The woman had already prepared food for them, water, some bread, and boiled eggs. "Outside, it was lightening up little by little, and everyone had started waking up for the day's activities. We started walking through the woods, towards the city, which was about six hours from the river," Precop said.

He told us that Ivan was very quiet. He was just answering the questions for half the way, and in the other half of the way he started telling the men how much he was thankful for this woman that helped him and became to him like a mother. She taught him how to read.

"Why don't you guys move to the city? Isn't it better?" asked Precop.

"We were both hurt by life, being around people; we both lost our families. Maybe next year, we'll talk about this," said Ivan.

"It's too dangerous to live in the woods," added the silent guy.

"You just have to believe that nobody will kill you," said Ivan, and he smiled at him.

"You always have to know for what and who you live! Look at this sun up there. Every day He is asking why do you live today? And you have to tell Him how much you love your life and for whom you live; you have to show Him the fire inside of you! And why do we live? Everyone decides for himself," continued Precop.

Ivan looked thoughtfully at him and asked, "Do you live for your family?"

"Yes," smiled Precop to him. "I miss them and I never lose hope. I miss them all. I did not see how they grew up; I have not seen them for almost nine years, but every day in my heart they are with me. They grow in my imagination. Pauline looks like my mom, Georgii like me, and Jacob like my wife." Precop smiled again and said, "My wife is like a sun, you look at her and she is smiling at you, no matter what, so feminine, so gentle, with a sober mind, and clean soul. Every morning she is praying and she is like a devoted soldier; you look at her and realize you cannot give up, you cannot lose your life, she is not letting you. I know now she is somewhere waiting for me, praying for me every day. And of course, she is fortune-telling, even if I forbade her to do this. She already knows or feels whether I will come to her or not."

Finally, they reached the river. "You just have to cross the river. After a few more days of walking you will get to the city. I will go back when the sun is up. And, yes, Precop, when I look for a wife, I want her to be like yours," Ivan said, and smiled at Precop.

Precop continued his story, "We got ready to cross the river. It was flowing very strongly. We secured our belongings to our backs and, little by little, we started swimming to the other side. The water was very cold, and the flow of the river was taking us away. We got to the other side with our last strength and we were breathing heavily. I looked across to check on Ivan, and we saw him playing with a stick on the other side. He had been waiting for us, for about forty-five minutes, till we got to the other side. He waved at us, signaling that he was leaving. At this moment, I saw a pack of wolves behind the boy. 'No! No!' I screamed with all my power. Birds flew from the trees. 'Wolves! Wolves! Look behind you. Wolves, please! Noo, please God, Nooo…!'"

He said his tears and yelling woke up all the forest inhabitants, but that didn't affect the wolves; their minds concentrated on pride. Ivan was looking at him and he couldn't hear, he just heard how Precop was trying to tell him something, but his words were muffled by the flow of the river. At the next moment, he turned his head to see all those wolves behind him. He threw the stick at them and started running to a tree. He had just grabbed the tree to climb it, and at the same time, one of the wolves jumped on his back and pulled him down. All the wolves attacked him and Ivan couldn't stand up again. Echoes of screaming surrendered to the whole forest.

From the other side, Precop screamed, "Nooo, God please no!" He started to swim back, but after a while, the boy's voice was no longer heard. He swam with all his power, but the river was taking him farther and farther and leaving him with no more strength. He had to turn back, for there was no point in dying. Precop came out of the water and just knelt with disappointment and looked at the sky. It was so cold, but he felt like he was burning with fire.

"Don't look; today's sky doesn't have your God," said the silent man. Precop just passed out. "Sometimes, we forget that we are made of flesh, so everything ends, like this sadness drowns in the river and looks around. Everything acts like nothing happened, even these birds who saw everything act like nothing happened; they just settled back in the trees," continued the silent man, talking to himself.

After a moment, Precop woke up from the cold. His body was hurting, he was moving little by little, and his tears came back to his eyes. The silent man didn't move from his place; he was just looking at the river and how beautiful it was in sunset light. Precop looked at him, then around, and sat down and was admiring the sunset that had just started. "All big feelings are burning to ashes: fire, life, death, love, betrayal, human birth, why? Is that to bring your soul to him? Is life a lesson for our soul? God, please don't leave me like this, in the mud with my sleeves dirty with dry human blood. I am scared, I am on the verge of losing my mind," prayed Precop.

"Precop, you still believe in God? He doesn't exist! Every day is darker than the night," said the silent man with a soft voice.

"I got it; you are the devil who is trying to kill the faith in me, but it is not going to happen, my friend!" Preop smiled with sarcasm and looked at him, "The sun is not rising without her praying to God for me and our kids; all the steps that I make are being committed into God's hands by her. For me to come to her, I hear it every time I want to release my soul to death. It doesn't matter how many times death has breathed on my back, but Maria has been in the gap postponing my last day."

The silent man insisted, "How do you control your mind? How do you find a middle between truth and delusion? It may interest you that if you go too far on truth, you may get disappointed in God, in your life, in any beliefs, and even in your mother that gave birth to you. But what if you go too far on delusion?" He stopped and made a thoughtful face. Precop continued, "If you go too far on delusion, you will go crazy and find the darkest hell inside of your inner mind, provided by your own mind. I've been there, trust me. It is so dark that till now I am not sure if you're real or I am just talking to myself." He smiled and made the silent man smile too.

They started walking. It was getting darker and darker and the city was farther than they thought. They just stopped and lit a fire with crackling wood and a dancing flame, which was like a lullaby, but they couldn't eat or sleep. "The desire that you are sincerely loved and expected is strong. This love doesn't exist; it is nine years and she forgot everything about you and got married to someone else a long time ago," said the silent man to Precop.

"No, I know her better than I know myself," smiled Precop. "I love her so much. Her beauty and inner beauty make me go deep inside of myself. This drive is priceless. This peace is eternal. I want to see her old, myself old, only beside her. This is the better gift from heaven that humans can have, the right person for themselves. You have to protect and appreciate her type because they are rare. Some people have it just like this. Some people fought for it, but if you find one, keep her protected, even from other women. Protect your woman, because time on earth is very short, even a hundred years is not enough for the right things." He smiled and looked in the sky full of stars. "Believing in love is the same thing as believing in God. You are not sure what it is, but you like it and you go for it. It feels good, feels like you don't know what can feel better.

The main thing is for people to prove their love and loyalty and this is so big that we humans want this. I know her, she will wait for me, and I want everything with her and nothing I want without her by my side. And if I made a mistake and she filled my spot beside her with someone else, I know she still loves me and I love her deeply too. And I will live with it, and that's enough for me."

The silent man looked at Precop, doubtful. "Fairy tales have to have a happy ending, but life sometimes gives you an unhappy one." Precop was picking at the fire with a stick and said quietly, "My world is better with her, and you know, I never have doubted the right path, because delirium is the one word that can accompany you, and you are afraid of it. Suddenly, delirium will get stuck like a bullet in the head and will not pass. So, let's believe in better, even though in bad is easier to believe."

The silent man was still looking at Precop and said, "Tell me more about your love. You know, at some point, something inside me started melting." He smiled. Precop smiled back at him and looked in his eyes. "Maria is my sun, night and day, she is so shiny in my eyes that I don't see anything else around that makes me more powerful, more loved, happier; she fills me. We don't have to talk sometimes. I remember her face and I want to breathe quietly, to not frighten her image. From my passion for her I could fly, it is so rare, the love that happened to me." He stopped for a moment, then continued, "I and Maria pray to one God, others even live in different worlds." Precop's eyes lit up like a candle and the silent man was looking at him and couldn't understand this fire of passion that Precop felt for his wife. "This woman has your soul for sure. You know, there is something in your love. I don't hear the screaming of that boy in my ears anymore, and at some point that crazy picture of the wolves ripping off a young body disappears somewhere. We got to the light, after the plunge into the ever-apparent darkness." Precop looked at him with tears. "Yes!"

They slept for a few hours. Early in the morning, the sun started breaking through the trees, bringing no happiness. Precop woke up the silent guy and they continued. They were tired, hungry, dirty, and almost there; they could hear the train nearby, people, noise, and barking dogs.

"Finally, we are here, which took me nine years. I got separated from my family. I couldn't come back to this point for so long. From here I have nowhere to go. It's like parting with your soul," said Precop, as he looked around. "Nothing changed; everything looks the same. I always imagined this place, how we met here; every day I have seen this city and place in my head."

"I will go and check around this area, look for work, food, and a place to stay overnight," said the silent guy. "Okay," replied Precop. His eyes were glued to the blue house; nine years ago, he told his family to come and stay, and he had always been waiting, and always hoping. He didn't know, back then, that he was asking for so much from those little kids and his beautiful wife. He didn't know that he was asking them for nine years, nine years of hope, prayer, patience, and suffering. He just realized now that he had asked for too much on that day. He started crying. He came close to that house. He looked around. He had told them every Friday, but it was only Monday.

People were going back and forth to work. He was totally exhausted and felt like his inside power was just enough for only one last breath. He said to himself, *I am scared that I am far away from you Maria. I am scared that I will not find you! I am scared that we will go through the same road, but at different times.* Precop's mind was playing with him in different ways. Throughout the day, he went back and forth around the city and there was no news about Maria, nobody to ask, or who knew her. The silent man came to Precop in the evening. "Did you find her?" Precop smiled hopelessly. "It's a simple question but has to be answered through an upside-down soul."

"No!" The silent man put his hand on his shoulder. "I found a church here; they can let us sleep there. They may have some bread to offer us, and then tomorrow we will look again!" While they were walking to this church, the silent man tried to make Precop feel better. "Maybe I am an empty, lost soul for you, but you wake up something holy in me. You're making me better; you make me believe in people when I lost this belief a long time ago. I think this is one of a human's tasks in life, to change people around them and make them better! I think you shared too much with me and now we have to be friends," the silent man said, smiling. Precop looked at him and said, "I don't know. Are you sure you're not one of the bad friends?" Precop pushed him a little, jokingly.

"Why? There are 'bad friends' too?" asked the silent man, confused.

"Ha-ha, yes, you know, those who are waiting for you to fall, smiling and coming to your house, eating with you at the same table, but their minds are filled up with evil because you're better than them. It's like having the devil's hand on your shoulder and you don't know," continued Precop.

The silent man became serious and couldn't say anything for a while, then he broke the silence. "I am a good friend. I don't know what you passed through, but I know myself. I know who I am and I know that I am a good person. Even though I don't believe in God, actually with you I've made up my mind to believe in something more than just life on earth. Also, there has appeared a desire to believe in love and friends. Also, with a good friend, you can achieve more, and go farther in life. If he is smarter, it is better for you because you are with him and he can advise you. Also, you're not God. You need advice too, even though you're asking God for advice, and God is still answering you through your best friend."

Precop looked at him and smiled. "Definitely!" They asked the church for lodging for a night or two. They gave them a corner and two blankets, and they went to sleep.

In a short while, a new day, a new morning, and new sunrise arrived, brightening the whole environment. Precop was awake and the silent man woke up too. "She is here," said Precop. "I sensed her smell. I saw a dream, and she came to this church." The silent man looked at him and said, "You're just crazy!" He brought some food that the church shared with them. "I can't do anything else today. I am going to look for her," said Precop. The silent man replied, "It's totally fine. You look bewitched and I don't think you can do anything else. It's all right, I will look for work for both of us."

Throughout the day, Precop was looking around and again he decided to sit a little bit on the bench by the blue house there. He got tired. He didn't eat anything for the whole day, so he put his head down and closed his eyes. He saw this picture from nine years ago, again and again. After a while, he felt that somebody sat by him. He raised his head and looked to the side, and there was a beautiful young girl with blue eyes and blond, long, curly hair looking at him. "Are you hungry?" asked the girl with her sweet voice. Precop couldn't say anything; he was ashamed to tell her that he was, and also, he had the feeling that he was seeing someone familiar, and inside of him was blooming happiness. "No, thank you," he answered, after he stood up and left. He went back to church. He was asking himself, *Who is this little angel?* For a while he thought maybe this didn't even happen; he had just been crazy because he hadn't eaten well for a long time.

"I have good news, I found someone who can help us make new passports, with a different name, and also, I found a job for us! Here is a guy, a church clerk. Precop are you okay?" said the silent man. "You have to eat, my friend. Look, I brought some food, Precop, and did you hear what I just told you? Why are you not saying anything? You look like you saw a ghost." He put his hand on Precop's shoulder and handed him a bowl of soup that he got from the church. Precop said, "I saw a girl, a young girl, she filled me with hope and happiness, she looked so familiar to me." The silent man sat down by him against the wall and started eating. "Did you talk to her? What did she say?"

Precop looked at him, smiling with tears. "She didn't say anything, but she looked like my mother! I couldn't say a word either, for the first time in my life," said Precop. The silent man said, "So, I can't understand. Is this a sign, from your God? What does that mean? I think you have to slow down, you're getting crazier. Please eat and stop scaring me, because I don't see any angels up there, only mud and gray people with sad faces."

The next day was a big holiday. It didn't matter how this new day would be, the only thing that was beautiful for him on this day and the reason he arose, was that there was another day closer to Maria.

Precop was ready to go out and there he saw two women by the church, speaking about something quietly and laughing. They brought some food, fruits, cookies, and wine to church. He tried to see their faces but he couldn't. The women put their scarves on their heads and went inside the church. It was too early and the church was empty, except for those women, and it was full of crackling candles all around. Precop went inside and tried from the other side of the church to look at them, but something inside him made him go after them.

When he got inside and saw their faces, he recognized Maria. She looked so good, so beautiful, and so happy. The sun from the windows was lighting her face. She hadn't changed, she looked even better. He said to himself, *Oh my God! I found her, she is here, in the same building as me. I look so bad, and how I can tell her that I am here? She is so happy. What if she is married? What if she has somebody else, and a new family? How can I tell her I am here?* He was looking at her beautiful body, her hands, her gentle smile, and her face, her hair that was showing from under the scarf, and little wrinkles under her eyes when she smiled. He was hiding and looking at her, like a stranger. He was scared to take his eyes from her, he was scared that he was going to lose her again, and at the same time, he did not dare to come close to her to speak.

After a few hours of watching her, the church had filled to the brim with people and it was harder to see her. Precop came closer. He stood behind her, inhaling her nice smell. He wanted to scream with happiness, he wanted to hug her, kiss her, and never let her go. But what if she had another family? His mind was hurting his soul.

He couldn't hold in his feelings and the desire of touching her again. He came closer to her, and from the back he took her right hand, passing his fingers between her fingers, and he hugged her from the back with his left hand around her left shoulder. He used to hug her every time like this when he was with her.

Maria put her left hand on his hand and closed her eyes with tears, which made her body cold in a moment. She put her head down and without looking behind her, she started crying. Her legs could not hold her, and she fell on her knees, and together with Precop, cried too. Vera, Maria's' friend, was looking at them with her hand covering her mouth, smiling and so happy for Maria. From the other side, the silent man was looking and couldn't believe his eyes. "Wow, he found her," said the silent man, shaking his head.

"Maria, I am here for you," said Precop with a quiet voice. She turned her head to him; she couldn't recognize him, he looked so old. His face was wrinkled and he was so thin. His eyes were sunken and his body was just bones. He looked so tired, with a beard, and his hair unkempt, with torn clothes, and in some places the clothes were shredded, just threads. She looked at him, they stood up, she hugged him more and more. She couldn't believe it.

He tried to stop her. He was feeling very guilty that he had taken so much time to come to her. He didn't have anything with him to give her, just love. Maria's eyes were sparkling like two stars and she was looking at him with complete happiness. Precop didn't know that she had all their children with her and they were all waiting only for him.

They went outside the church. "Maria, you look, so good," said Precop, touching her face. "It's like a dream," he continued. He was holding her hands. He kissed her wrist. He used to kiss her wrist every time before, saying, "My angel and I kissed in the holy place." They couldn't stop looking at each other. "Maria, I will never leave you, because the last time I left you, and after I separated from you, days and nights were like long nights with all nightmares. Maria, I went through hell," said Precop and hugged her again.

"Precop, I was looking for you too, and your face was hiding in every window, in everyone passing by; you were somewhere nearby all the time. Let's go home," said Maria. Precop looked at her. "Home?" She smiled. "Yes, home." They were holding hands; they had so much to tell each other, but the power of happiness that was boiling inside of them, the big feeling, was so good that it kept them quiet. Soon, they got to the blue house and Maria was opening the small gate.

"Maria, you rented a house. Where did you get money for the rent?" She looked at him and smiled, saying, "Precop, I bought this house." He asked, "Maria, how?"

He couldn't believe that Maria bought the house after waiting for him so long. This was his woman. "Precop, this house was going to be mine from the day we separated. After I moved in, I never locked the door, and it was unlocked every day, waiting for you to open it, for so many years."

They went inside and Maria was holding his hand. Inside, he was very surprised and shocked because he saw there the young girl who had offered him food outside; she was cooking. The girl turned around and recognized him too. She looked at Maria. "Mom, this is the man that I was telling you about." Maria jumped with a smile and said, "Pauline, this is your father." She came slowly to him and hugged him softly. "The food is almost ready, take a seat!"

Precop's tears were flowing from his very serious face and he said, "Please, forgive me, Maria." His voice was trembling, he looked at the window, he saw the bench outside, and he realized that Maria was waiting in that place, looking out the window every day. "I feel like two different lives met in this short day, today," he said, then he paused. "We will reaffirm our love, Maria!" He stood up, kissed her hand and lips, then kissed Pauline's forehead, and looked at her eyes. "You look like my mother and your mother! You are so beautiful?" He sat back, put his hands on the table, put his head on his hands, and started crying like a child. Maria and Pauline became worried and hugged him from both sides.

After he calmed down, Pauline started putting the food on the table. "Soon, they will come too and we can eat together," said Pauline. "Who? Who else is living here?" asked Precop. Maria looked at him and took his hand. "Our boys, Precop, everyone is here, only you were delayed. We all were waiting for you," said Maria. They ate. Precop couldn't wait to see his boys and wondered how they looked.

He said, "Maria, you always were like a bright light in the darkness on my way here. Nothing could break me; you were giving me this power, even when death breathed on my back, you felt it, you would pray it away from me. You're my power till the end of my life. Maria, you're bigger than God for me. At some point in my life, I thought that God didn't exist, but because I have you, I was still trusting Him, trusting that the way and path I was going would bring me to you. We were far from each other, but our time flew together. I didn't keep track of the days; for the last few years, I was just like a lost soul who was waiting for the moment of our meeting."

Maria is an example of the perfect woman of all time. But who made her like this? The love of her man. Deep love and care made a young woman into a strong woman who was fully hidden in God.

In a while, Georgii and Jacob came home. Georgii opened the door and he saw Precop. "Father," he ran and hugged him, and Jacob did the same after. Georgii was taller than Precop. Georgii was repeating, "Father,

Father," but couldn't finish the sentence, just pronouncing "Father." He was looking into his eyes and it was as if they were talking to each other through their eyes. They were very close to each other, from the day of Georgii's birth.

They stayed all night together, all the family, again together. They couldn't get enough of each other, and they were laughing, crying, and then staying silent. Emotions of love and happiness, and peaceful feelings filled each of them. They were looking at each other with happiness and appreciation. They had each other and they were blessed to have stayed alive and to have found each other. It was so very rare to survive with the whole family in those days.

Money and wealth didn't matter to them. They were happy when they had everything and when they had nothing but a piece of bread and a bowl of soup that was divided into five.

The next day, Precop talked to the silent guy to make a passport for everybody, with a different last name, so they could go home. The government at this time had calmed down a little bit because they had lost a lot of people.

Precop also gave the silent man money. "Where did you get the money from?" he asked. Precop replied, "I changed it on the first day when we got here, from gold teeth that I took from dead bodies while I was burying them in the ground for all those nine years. A lot of people were wealthy, so almost every dead body that passed through my hands had gold teeth. And it was a good amount." The silent man looked at him and smiled. "Oh, my good brother, I thought you were a holy person." He tapped him a few times on the shoulder, smiling as a joke.

"Doesn't have anything to do with it," said Precop very seriously. "There are some for you too. I am not going to ask what you're going to do, or where you're going to go after this, but I wish you a "sun woman" and deep love." Precop smiled. The silent man looked in the sky and it was cloudy because it was about to rain. He said, "It seems to me, that I don't deserve it. This is too expensive a gift that heaven can give."

Precop saw Vera walking and pointed at her with his chin. "They're only clouds of rain and you don't see the sun, but it is right there!"

***

A lot of suicides, a high rate of kids' mortality, the government couldn't control, and four million innocent people were sent into taiga for no reason. The law did not allow you to return home, but this was my only dream, to come back where I belonged for every feast.

"Precop," Maria interrupted him from deep thinking. "Everything is good. Why are you sad?" He looked at her and hugged her. "Maria, I am afraid of everything now. I have so much in my hands, you, our kids, and I realize that I did everything right when I brought you here. I left you because we couldn't all run together at that moment when they saw us; it was too late. My decision on that day wasn't a choice, it was our last chance of staying alive. I gave hope to my family. I gave myself to them to take the attention from you. I am sorry Maria, but this was one of the best decisions in my life. It was very hard for you and our kids, but you cannot imagine what real hell others went through. I have met cannibalism. People were starving. It was better to be in the dark with beasts, than endure this pain between people. When they brought me back, a big epidemic hit the children. I have witnessed so many scary pictures and so much pain, Maria."

After a silent minute he continued, "When I ran away for the second time, I stumbled across a bunch of dead children in the woods. I was alone, my soul froze at the sight of those dead innocent children. Even the air was dead there. They laid there with white faces and hands of frozen blood on the damp ground. Even the animals in the forest felt that pain and were staying away from that place. I wasn't waiting for the morning, I got used to it like a beast in the dark forest. I couldn't feel pain and didn't expect changes. I had nothing to keep my soul warm at that moment. My eyes were frozen too. I fell on my knees and I didn't know what to do. There was no time to bury them. I started praying, but my prayer was so empty, with no signs or belief in God."

His nose was running, his tears came faster from his eyes, he wiped his face again and looked at Maria with the face and eyes of a little child. "Maria, you saved me! Right in that moment and other hard moments, you saved me! Such sacrifice was enough to remember your face and add sunrise to it, our garden, and our house. I immediately saw myself in a warm nice place. It was like wings to me, that it was really like a game, every time like a game with my mind. There was no other way out, otherwise, I would have to lose my mind. For all these years in a row, I didn't want to remove any pain or look for pleasure or something pleasant. I was just thinking of peace." Maria hugged him tighter and he said, "Time seems to be running out inside me, not outside." They stayed like this for hours.

After several months, we finally got our passports. We sold the little blue house in a corner of a small city and left the place forever. We left that city with the new last name of "Roshko" and the new life in the old place.

In a few weeks, with train and horse carriage, we reached home. Our village looked so different. Ten years had passed and everything was so different. Then another grief hit us. Our mothers both had passed away. We settled in my mother's house. In our house, where we used to live before, other people had occupied it. Precop really wanted this house back, because this house was so beautiful, as if he'd breathed life into every stone. We had to buy this house at three times more in price. The lands were taken by the government, but we were happy that at least we could have our house and the little garden beside it.

People were scared. They give responsibility for themselves to politicians, saying, "As you say, so we will;

what you will feed, we will eat." People no longer wanted to get out of the general rules, they just wanted to be left alone, they just wanted peace and nothing else. People were like paralyzed consciousness; they were like zombies. They weren't even searching for absolution. They spoke little to each other, met each other little, they were just afraid.

***

The peace and silence were no longer visible. On September 1, 1939, the beginning of the war was declared. The war of two world military-political coalitions became the largest armed conflict in the history of mankind- Germany and the Soviet Union.

Well, that's another heavy, long story, but all I can say about it is that my sons returned with medals and we were really proud of them. Precop and I lived to a ripe old age.

You cannot deny your fate, but being in the power of love, you can save your life. Faith and love alone can bring you out of the darkness. Also, you have nothing in this galaxy but your life and your love for something or someone. This power is strengthening you to continue the lost path.

About Kharis Publishing:

Kharis Publishing, an imprint of Kharis Media LLC, is a leading Christian and inspirational book publisher based in Aurora, Chicago metropolitan area, Illinois. Kharis' dual mission is to give voice to under-represented writers (including women and first-time authors) and equip orphans in developing countries with literacy tools. That is why, for each book sold, the publisher channels some of the proceeds into providing books and computers for orphanages in developing countries so that these kids may learn to read, dream, and grow. For a limited time, Kharis Publishing is accepting unsolicited queries for nonfiction (Christian, self-help, memoirs, business, health and wellness) from qualified leaders, professionals, pastors, and ministers. Learn more at: About Us - Kharis Publishing - Accepting Manuscript